Frank Alper

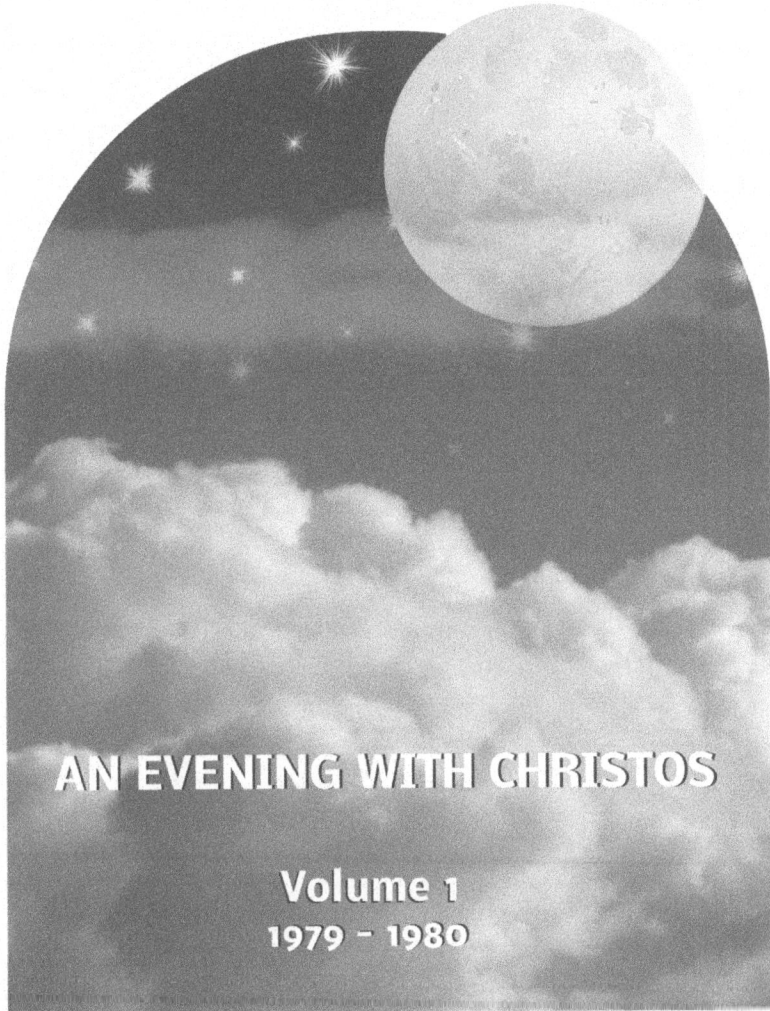

AN EVENING WITH CHRISTOS

Volume 1
1979 - 1980

Imprint
Copyright © 2024 ADAMIS - Katharina Alper
An Evening with Christos
Frank Alper
ISBN 978-3-9526044-2-7

Edition ADAMIS
Katharina Alper
Zwydenweg 14
CH 6052 Hergiswil NW Switzerland

Phone: 0041 41 630 33 01
Email: katharina.alper@adamis.ch
Website: www.adamis.ch

Channeled through Rev. Dr. Frank Alper 1980
Volume 1 (of 5) Original transcripts of the evening sessions from
Sept. 1978-Dec. 1979
Editor: Katharina Alper
Layout: Katharina Alper
Cover design: Katharina Alper

Background and Source Material

Dr. Frank Alper: A spiritual teacher who transitioned in 2007, leaving behind numerous manuscripts and recordings from over 30 years of lectures and seminars.

Channeling Sessions: The books "Moses and the Bible" and "An Evening with Christos" are based on channeling sessions conducted by Dr. Alper in Phoenix, Arizona, in the late 1970s and early 1980s.

Content and Authenticity

Transcripts: These books contain original transcripts from the channeling evenings.

Maintaining Originality: The transcripts preserve the original spoken words, even if they sometimes deviate from correct grammar. This decision ensures that the unique energy and essence of the messages are maintained.

Purpose and Usage

Energy and Wisdom: The words are not just informational but also sources of spiritual energy. Each channeled message carries the unique energy of the entity being channeled.

Reading Experience: Readers are encouraged to read the books aloud or silently, feeling the energy of the words and allowing them to resonate personally.

Interpretation: The sentences are complex and open to multiple interpretations. Readers should contemplate and find the aspects of the truth that resonate with them.

Editorial Notes

Typographical Errors: While efforts were made to correct typographical errors, some may remain due to the volume of material.

Recommendation: Readers should approach the books with an open mind, allowing the channeled words to inspire and guide them.

The original transcripts aim to provide a direct and authentic connection to Dr. Alper's spiritual teachings, offering inspiration and personal spiritual experiences.

We wish you freedom, joy and happiness in your life.

Edition Adamis, Katharina Alper

Table of Contents

Chapter 16

Frank Alper

Frank Alper: A Journey of Spiritual Discovery

Frank Alper was born on January 22, 1930, into a traditional Jewish family in Brooklyn, New York. From a young age, Frank questioned the traditions of his faith. During the ten days of repentance between Rosh Hashanah and Yom Kippur, he listened to the long list of sins he was accused of committing and couldn't understand how he could be guilty of sins he did not even comprehend. This experience sparked a lifelong quest to understand the nature of sin, God, and the Creator.

As he matured, Frank felt increasingly restless and unhappy within his tradition. His longing for deeper insight and wisdom became almost unbearable. In the 1970s, driven by his search for truth, Frank moved to Phoenix, Arizona, leaving behind his family, friends, job, and a comfortable life. With just a suitcase and a heart full of determination, he started anew, committed to finding the right answers and achieving inner peace.

During this period, Frank underwent what he referred to as his "initiations of fire," which connected him profoundly to Universal Law and solidified his integrity. His strong connection to the lost civilization of Atlantis led him to channel a body of work titled "Exploring Atlantis" in the early 1980s. This work focused on crystals and their geometric configurations and became central to his seminars.

What began with a handful of students quickly blossomed into a movement. Frank's teachings on crystal energy and his healing methods spread rapidly across North America. Affectionately known as "Crystal Daddy" by his followers, Frank's channeling sessions were renowned for their accuracy. Often, the profound truths he conveyed took time for individuals to fully integrate, revealing their significance only in retrospect.

Frank's teachings centered on the belief that all humans are children of the universe, capable of achieving anything. He emphasized that our purpose on Earth is to have spiritual experiences that expand our consciousness through the duality and freedom of life. "Your existence is mind," he often said, "and through your mind, you can create any reality you wish."

For over three decades, Frank shared his vast reservoir of spiritual knowledge and healing methods across North America, Europe, and Japan. As a universal channel, he introduced his students to a multitude of entities, masters, angels, and abstract energies. His strong connection to Moses led to the channeling of the "Spiritual Numerology of Moses," a system now known as the Soul Plan.

In the early 1980s, Frank began channeling information about the "children of the new root race," later known as Indigo or Crystal Children. He described these children with different color qualities and assigned them specific guardians, potentials, and tasks. This foresight into a new generation highlighted his role as a pioneer.

Frank's innovative spirit also led to the development of ENERGENETICS, a method of genetic energy reconstruction aimed at eradicating genetic conditions. Although not yet widely practiced, Frank believed this method would one day help reduce genetic illnesses, aligning with his belief that the right person would always emerge to introduce crucial advancements to humanity.

Despite the breadth of beings Frank channeled, his most significant goal was to help individuals achieve emotional freedom and balance their soul existence with earthly life. This vision guided his teachings until the very end.

In 2005, aware of his declining health, Frank referred to this period as his "final chapter." His faith in God and spirit remained unshakable, even as he sensed his days were numbered. He taught with renewed urgency, delivering his last seminar in Switzerland in October 2007. Frank Alper passed away in Switzerland on December 7, 2007, at the age of 77, leaving behind a legacy of spiritual enlightenment and healing.

Introduction to Volume 2

Rev. Dr. Frank Alper: Evenings session under the Titel of "An Evening with Christos" from January until December 1980

Seventeen months ago, I was requested by Spirit to conduct a monthly channeling session for truth, growth, and love. The words written in this book are my truth. I do not ask the readers to accept them as their truth. I only ask your indulgence, and an open, searching mind to consider my words and discern your truth.

The book follows my own enlightenment. In the earlier sessions many of the lectures are from my spiritual Masters. At this time all communication is relayed consciously from my soul. It is not my purpose to make predictions, nor to involve anyone in psychic vibrations.

All transmissions are designed to be presented totally in spiritual vibrations for growth. I give you the following pages in love and humility. I am eternally grateful to our Father for allowing me to serve my brothers and sisters in this capacity.

In Love and Light, Rev. Dr. Frank Alper

Chapter 1

Sananda: Spaceships

Bless you, My Children. We are Sananda.

Once again, we welcome you within the vibrations of this home, this sanctuary.

We are now currently in the month of the change of the seasons, the Augusta of the Fall. It is indeed time to reap the efforts of much hard work, sacrifice, and suffering that has taken place in the past several months.

The culmination of the work and the tasting of the fruit from the vine shall begin to occur for most of you toward the end of this month. Beginning in the month of October many things shall manifest themselves to you at the conscious level, to put aside any doubts that you may have had in your minds as to your Father's true Purpose for the suffering and the trials you have undergone to this point.

I speak to you tonight in an area relating to your space brothers and sisters who have journeyed for many years, and some who are still in the throes of journey at this time to place themselves at strategic points within the outer perimeters of this planet.

There are at this time approximately 137,000 alien souls incarnated on the planet Earth in physical form. They have spent many years in preparation for the environmental adjustment necessary to survive on the planet. They are here to help, to teach, to assist the Children of Light, such as yourselves, in furthering your Father's Work on this planet. There are four such souls in attendance in the room this evening.

Before the end of the year there will be several landings of ships on the surface of this planet. This will be done to allow certain selected Children of Light to be elevated into the confines of a vehicle for study and purification. The process will only take several hours. Then those chosen will return, never again to be as they were before their journey. For at that time, they shall be pure of mind, body and spirit, so that the three facets of the individual shall undergo a supreme blending into one, to one totally spiritual being with an aura bordering on white, and a vibration of purity.

These journeys shall be spaced and timed at similar intervals at various points throughout the world. In the spring of the year 1980, it is planned that the first public landing of a special vehicle shall be made. It shall not be a surprise but shall be planned through official government channels with propriety and dignity. This shall be a monumental occasion and a major breakthrough for God, for by that time the spiritual awakening that is coming to fruit at the present time throughout the world shall have begun to blossom and flourish in vast numbers.

The ship chosen to land for the first recognition is named Jupiter I. The ship is equivalent in size to a building of thirty-seven stories in height and has a capacity of 9,600 people. If the balance of the energies does not continue to increase and develop as is currently taking place, if the negativity is not transmuted into love, then we shall have to postpone the landing. Know that despite the importance of this event, we must allow for the free will of the soul.

In the year of 1985, it will become quite noticeable that there are physical changes occurring within the surface of the structure of this planet. These changes have already begun to occur in minor degrees.

It is not our Divine Father's desire, nor plan, to destroy this planet and all the souls inhabiting it. The changes that will occur are a normal, maturing, shifting result of the growth of this Universe, and particularly this Solar System.

All things occur as they must. Those who walk in the Light have nothing to fear. They are, in truth, guided by their Divine Father. There have been many stories and predictions made relating to the destruction of this planet, to the mass slaughter of hundreds of millions of souls. I do not give credibility to, nor deny these stories. It is not a necessity on my part to account for our Father's Actions, only to have faith in His wisdom. And so, I ask you all not to walk or conduct your lives in fear and apprehension. Bless your Father when you rise in the morning for the day of life that lies ahead of you and lead it in love and peace and growth. Know that your needs truly will be cared for.

Certain among you in this room shall begin to receive communication from Jupiter I within the next six or seven weeks. It will begin the planning and the study necessary for you, along with the knowledge for you to share with others. It will pertain to descriptions of the ship, its purposes, and what you must do in preparation for the coming event. Those of you who shall serve in this capacity shall be notified a few days before by one of your Masters so that you may prepare yourselves properly for the communication.

Questions and Answers

Now you may proceed with the period of questioning.

Question: Is the Jupiter I in close orbit around this planet, and have I been observing it for a number of years?

Answer: At times her orbit brings her fairly close to this planet, and at other times quite far away. You have on occasion, been in communication with this ship.

Question: Is the ship that rises shortly after sunset, in the west just off the horizon, Jupiter I?

Answer: The ship you refer to is called the Golden Eagle.

Question: Is it also called the Dove, or ship #10?

Answer: The ship known as the Dove is located more into the southwest than west directly.

Question: Is it the brightest appearance before any other star appears?

Answer: Yes.

Question: What significance does K35 play? We had a sighting about three years ago at the four peaks area.

Answer: You are referring to a ship known as Dragon Three. This ship has been in orbit around the Earth for 134 years. It has been a primary factor in supplying certain energy centers in this area with high concentrations of energy and power.

Question: Where did you say Jupiter I would land in the U.S.?

Answer: I did not say, My Child. It is known, but at this point and time we shall pass on that question.

Question: When I self-realized in 1973, or what I call self-realization, I was shown that there are over ten million spaceships over planet Earth and in our Solar System ready for any eventuality. My understanding also was that there are as many as there are ships and humans on planet Earth. I read an article today in a newspaper that states that there are over ten million aliens in the U.S. I have a prior feeling of six million. Is that correct?

8

Answer: It is at this present time slightly overstated. Once again, I say to you that many things that have already occurred within the spiritual vibrations have not yet actually come to realization within the physical energies. Time discrepancy has long been a problem in communication. I will say that within time those figures shall approach the truth.

Question: What is the name of the ship circling the moon about seventeen years fourth of the size of the moon itself?

Answer: The name of the ship is Jupiter III.

Question: Was the ship on any special mission?

Answer: To assist its brothers on a project inside the core of the moon itself.

Question: What purpose does the alphabet have with Jupiter I?

Answer: It is their language, and therefore, their method of communication. The Jupiterian alphabet has been related to you through your spiritual writing so that it may be dispersed to a selected few for study and assimilation. It will make communication, writing and reading of material interchangeable and easily understood. You do not realize what a monumental event occurred during that transmission.

Question: When anyone channels, are these channels to be

taken seriously by that person and worked with? Does it matter if someone else receives a different channeling?

Answer: Within the course of time, certain channels shall fall by the wayside, or shall advance their vibrations to the higher rays to achieve direct communication without distortion. We do not mean to infer that a channel is supplying misguided information, nor untruths. Unfortunately, many times, in the shifting of energy patterns, the lowering of levels in order to establish communication causes a

9

loss of original context of wordage and meaning. This situation is rapidly being corrected. All those who serve as channels have already begun to experience, or shall experience shortly, energizing. This will raise the levels of vibrations within them to enable them to channel directly. This shall eliminate much confusion that has manifested itself up to this time.

Question: Will you share with us the names of the aliens in the room?

Answer: I do not feel that it is my right to do so. Each individual will react differently to this announcement. Those who are, know they are. At their own discretion and comfort, they may announce it.

Question: Concerning my involvement with the fulfillment of the Hopi legends, and that current project, there seems to be a problem within the structure of the Mormon organization concerning their eventual caretaking of the land that the Hopi now occupy. What avenues might be used to further their cooperation and eventual harmonious proceeding into the slot they are supposed to fill?

Answer: There will, of necessity, have to be a concession made to those affiliated with the Mormon Church in order to gain their acceptance and willingness to cooperate totally with you in this project. It will relate to possession of certain areas of information that will be uncovered, more in the capacity of one hand washing the other. The two of you cannot enter into this project with closed minds heading forward in one direction only. You must be flexible and willing to bend, keeping in mind that the ultimate goal is the realization of the project. The road travelled may not be to your liking, but it will lead you to the goal. Be flexible, and it shall go well.

Question: What should I do with the knowledge of the magnets and the crystals?

Answer: At this time, assimilate and correlate them into a discourse and a scientific journal report. Keep them, for the time is not yet right for them to be released, as the energies would fall on deaf ears at this time.

Question: When I get my information on the tablets, can I bring along one or two to assist me?

Answer: There has been no projected manifested, or that shall manifest where one Child of Light shall be requested to travel and complete a mission by itself. We do not wish to chance failure. All projects shall have those with a prime responsibility, and those who shall assist and aid their energies to its completion.

Question: What are the purposes for the various generating plants beneath the Earth that have argon gas in them?

Answer: We cannot discuss this at this time.

Question: How much truth has been written into the Bible, in reference to the Creator, relating to His wrath?

Answer: When you read your Bible, read it with your heart and your soul. The words that impress themselves upon your conscious mind, that seem to be true: believe. The words that express things that you cannot accept within your truth, reject, and then you shall have your truth.

Question: In a prior channeling, we were told that until this fall we will still receive names so we can orient ourselves better. There is an entity in this room who just spoke. Did we have anything to do with Montezuma's Castle? Is there any information we have to retrieve from there? It seems to me that I have been kept out of there more than once. I don't know why. Possibly it was not time yet?

Answer: There is and has been a powerful negative field of energy manifesting itself at the place you refer to as Montezuma's Castle. The time will come when this energy field shall be dispersed. At that time, you will uncover much information there. There are things necessary for you to recover and study. For now, wait. You shall be informed when the time is proper.

Question: I have in mind to send our vibrations to the meeting which is taking place with the heads of state in the U.S. at this time, to send our energies in their direction to keep it a peaceful endeavor. Are there any particular suggestions we might get for that purpose?

Answer: All those who desire to participate in such an effort are truly blessed. Place yourselves in circles of not less than three and solidify the energies flowing throughout the circle. Send the energies of peace and unity to those heads of state currently in conference. All shall come to pass, and peace shall reign. We Bless you for your thoughts in that direction.

We take this opportunity to close this session. We cover you all with the energies of your Divine Father, and We Bless you, each one. God Bless you all.

Chapter 2

Michael: The Energies of Sananda, and the Christ Spirit

Good evening, my fellow Children of Light. This is Michael speaking to you.

Tonight, I shall begin the discussion, for you must understand that this soul is composed of the energies of Michael, Sananda, and the Christ Spirit.

There are many new vibrations in this room tonight, and yet they are all familiar to us. The topic for discussion tonight relates primarily to the utilization of the knowledge of our space brothers on Jupiter I to assist you in fulfilling your destinies, and in doing God's Work on the Earth plane.

In order to avoid any confusion or the slightest distortion of a word, a thought, a vibration, we are going to allow the energies of Murvin, commander of Jupiter I, to channel through us directly this night. The voice shall be mine, for we no longer are permitted any outside direct channeling to occur.

Murvin: Commander of Jupiter I

Good evening, my brothers and sisters. This is Murvin speaking to you from Jupiter I. You cannot imagine what an honor and a pleasure it is for me to be able to do this, not only on this night, but to do it at all. I have waited many, many years for this opportunity to speak, and indeed it is my honor to do so. We here on Jupiter I have been in orbit around the planet Earth for over 474 of your years. Our work has been long and tedious in preparation for perhaps this very night, to be able at last to establish a solid link of communication with you so that we may plan accordingly for the salvation of the planet Earth.

There are, from the complement of this ship, 2,447 souls incarnated on your planet at this time. The balance remains on board, making a total complement of 9,600 assigned to Jupiter I. All of the incarnated souls are in various countries and societies throughout your world. Within the next five years, all incarnated souls from Jupiter I shall have total consciousness of the origin of their souls. Most of them, at this time, are consciously aware of their spiritual development and abilities, but are not aware of their origin.

There are tonight an additional three alien souls in this room. This makes a total of seven, three of which are from Jupiter I. When all are made aware of their origin, communication links shall be established between these souls and the ship to enable them to understand and spread the word in relation to plans pertaining to increasing spacial and Earth communication.

There will be a pilot landing toward the end of this month. We are forbidden to say when, or whom shall be taken aboard. I am sorry, but it must be this way on the first ascent to avoid mass confusion, as we know in our hearts that you all wish to make the journey.

We are shortly going to begin to transmit to certain channels whose vibrations we are compatible with the characters and symbols that formulate our language. It truly bears no relationship to your language. Our letters or characters are composed of what you refer to as geometric symbols. It was designed this way for specific reasons. The interlacing of triangular, circular, and rectangular symbols manifests a certain level and color of energy. This enables us, with our language, to communicate directly at great distances in energy form. Part of the purpose for teaching you our language is to enable you to utilize this tool, and to possibly understand how to alter and symbolize your own language, thus giving you the same abilities for space communication.

We serve here, at this present time, as an intermediate relay station for many of the high-level energies that were given to the care of Evangeline by our Divine Father. We have, through this soul, enabled others to begin to utilize and draw these energies to themselves. These higher levels of energy are indeed the vibrations relating to spacial communication, and to cellular and atomic healing. Or, as you refer to on Earth, regeneration of bone and tissue.

If you will all close your eyes and open your spiritual chakras to receive my spiritual energies, I shall open a channel to each of you, a channel of vibration enabling you, if you so desire, to communicate with my energies when there is a true need for you. Let us do that now, please... It is done, my brothers and sisters. And now I step aside, for there is someone else who wishes to speak to you. I am available for questioning when that period commences.

My beloved Children, this is your Divine Father speaking to you. Please send him all the energy you can, for this is a most difficult transmission for him.

All over this world, all over this Universe, all over the millions of Universes throughout creation beloved Children are sitting in circles such as this, sitting to pray for the growth of their souls, to seek direction to help all those who are lost to find their path back to eternal love. Your planet, within a period of six or seven years, shall undergo certain changes in its surface structure as part of a periodic cleansing and cyclic evolution. Devote your energies, whenever possible, to helping those who are lost to find their path, to open their hearts and their eyes so that they too may survive the changes that shall occur. The planet is destined to be a spiritual planet ruled by brotherhood and by love, for the souls that inhabit it are approaching the point within their development to achieve total fifth-level consciousness. Those of you who have not at this time begun your spiritual cleansing shall do so before this year passes into history. This will allow total union with your souls. For you, and untold thousands like you throughout the world, shall serve as the messengers, the messiahs, the disciples to aid your brothers and sisters. As I talk to you, each of you is being touched by the Light. It shall burn in your hearts for all eternity. My Divine Love and Blessings upon your souls.

Michael: Questions and Answers

This is Michael, My brothers and sisters.

It is time for the period of questioning. James shall act as monitor. You may direct your questions to Sananda, the Christ Spirit, Murvin, or Myself.

Question to Sananda: We received in the desert the time period of three weeks and three days toward the end of October, to pick up the tablets in the area designated to me to be given back to the Hopi. Is that date still standing?

Answer: The date stands without change.

Question to Sananda: Who shall receive the tablets of the Hopi, and where shall they be delivered?

Answer: The tablets shall be given to the one you refer to as Grandfather David at his place of residence.

Question to Sanada: Should we pick them up on the 10th day of October and deliver them the same day, or shall we show them first to the ones at the Focus?

Answer: Take the tablets directly to Grandfather David.

Question to Murvin: When you offered to open a channel to all of us here, I received an image of a male entity that was two-headed. Is that a correct image, or was I picking up on something else?

Answer: The image is indeed androgenous. The manifestation within your conscious mind was indeed two-headed to show you the duality of the energy vibrations.

Question to Murvin: When are the original letters of the alphabet going to be related to us?

Answer: We know you have suffered greatly with this, so we shall try to alleviate your concern as much as possible. The letters shall begin to come after four more of your philosophy lessons have been completed and tested.

Question to Murvin: I have a friend who letters now. Is he receiving letters from received nine letters so far.

Answer: He is receiving the letters from us.

Question to Sananda: Should I be involved in the Hopi situation?

Answer: It is not a necessity. If it is desired that your energies be added to the situation, they are surely welcome.

Question to Murvin: During the opening of the chakras, I received three syllables. I don't know if it is a name, or what. May I please have the meaning of Arh, Rrh, Mrh?

Answer: They are vibrational sounds similar to your usage of the Ohm. They have come to you, for this is the key to help you in opening your channels.

Question to Murvin: The spaceship I have been watching since 1973 called Jupiter #97, is that identified with your ship?

Answer: There are, all told, 368 ships that bear the name Jupiter. So, we say to you that Jupiter #97 most assuredly is within our complement and within our overall project.

Question to Murvin: There are a number of ships in fixed positions that I have seen and watched for a number of years right where I live. Are they all from the same galaxy?

Answer: Yes. They are a complement together.

Question to Sananda: Could you give us an estimated time between the day when original contact with the records shall be made?

Answer: It will be advisable to make this contact shortly before the sun rises in the morning.

Question to Sananda: This is the second time you have affirmed that we shall not be going to the Ruby Focus.

Answer: That is correct.

Question to Sananda: Should we document and film the entire operation?

Answer: By all means. However, when the filming and documentation is done, keep it quite well hidden until the time is proper to release it to the general public.

Question to Sananda: These records that are going back, will they only be the plaques, or will the other two pieces that are missing be returned at the same time?

Answer: The other two pieces that are missing should be returned at the same time.

Question to Sananda: Is this schedule, after the return of the plaques, to prepare the Hopi for the climbing of the rainbow staircase?

Answer: The Hopi shall not climb the rainbow staircase for at least three of their moons.

Question to Sananda: I also ask for some perception by you into the elders of the Mormon religion to qualify that their contact originally with the Hopi is more as an emissary of brotherly love than mission-ary. The Hopi will not receive them just as missionaries.

Answer: You have asked for the perception, and you shall receive it.

Question to Sananda: I have also received stimulation relating to the date, October 24th. Would you, at this time, clarify of what importance that date is to me?

Answer: The date, October 24th, will be a date that concrete information shall be shared with others, as well as yourself, relating to the journey that some will have made on a ship.

Question to Sananda: I would like some clarification. The answer was given that at sunrise contact shall be made. Does that refer to giving the tablets to the Hopi, or picking them up?

Answer: The tablets are to be picked up and delivered to the Hopi on the same day.

Question to Sananda: Is there any message for the Hopi?

Answer: It is important for all of you upon this trip to have walking with you all of the Masters you can summon, to have all of the energies of your brothers and sisters with you at this time so that all of you may indeed radiate Divine Light and Love. I do not have a specific message for the Hopi at this time. When the transfer is made then you shall give them a message from me.

Question to Sananda: Are these the same tablets that David asked me to look for and bring to him?

Answer: Yes.

Question to Murvin: will the full alphabet come this time, and what is its purpose?

Answer: In time the full alphabet shall come. The purpose for it has already been explained. Have patience, my child.

Question to Murvin: Some months ago, while I was channeling, I received some hand signals. Is this some type of communication?

Answer: Very definitely so. The hand signals are configurations and movements involving the fingers that generate certain levels and intensities of energy and direct them in specific directions. Many of these configurations will be taught to you in the future to help you control certain high levels of energy, to pinpoint their insertion in different types and methods of healing in addition to their use in communication.

Question to Sananda: I have information from a lady requiring some confirmation. She has offered the results of her channeling. I would like to verify her authenticity as a channel. I will say her name silently.

Answer: This is an authentic channel.

Question to Sananda: I was told by this channel that I will soon meet her son who is on board ship.

Answer: That is truth. His name is Ramen.

Question to Sananda: Is there any message for this lady? Answer: The only thing We can say is, bless her.

Question to Michael: Shall I be present at the finding of the tablets when they are to be picked up? Shall I continue on to be part of the delivery team?

Answer: Your vibrations and your energies touch all whom you meet. It will truly be a great asset for all to have you present throughout the course of this project.

Question to Michael: At this time, I have been wanting to further develop myself through the use of the awareness techniques. I feel at various times that I experience interference at various levels. Is this still going to be a problem for me?

Answer: The levels of your vibrations and energies are now higher than when you attempted this before. You do possess the ability to rise above the lower levels to achieve the communication with the higher levels of yourself. Try it again. It will certainly unlock the door to your development and communication with your higher self.

Question to Sananda: Are my energies needed on the Hopi mission?

Answer: It will suffice for you to send your energies and your love. It is not necessary that you physically involve yourself if your man desires that you do not do so.

Question to Murvin: I recently heard a piece of music. It came to me that the melody contains a mathematical equation of some sort. Are the numbers a formula to make the metal for the ships?

Answer: In part, your statement is correct. The energies of the music truly are in the form of an equation. However, they are not the formula for the metal used in the construction of the ships. The majority of the material used within the ships, specifically in the Jupiter fleet, is composed of an alloy, not only of metal but of plastisolids as well.

Question to Murvin: A few days ago, I saw a meteor in the east and a small bright one in the west. My impression was that they were ships and not meteors. Is that correct?

Answer: The one in the west was a meteor. The one in the east was Jupiter #43.

If there is not a question of great importance, we beg your indulgence and close the session for tonight, for indeed this vehicle is weary.

This is Michael. I Bless you all in our Divine Father's Light and Love. Let us all walk together for all eternity arm in arm, blending one with the other until the time comes when we are all as one again.

Chapter 3

Adamis

It is a pleasure to feel the energies of those who have not enhanced this circle before. We welcome them in our Divine Father's Light.

It has indeed been, for many of you, quite a strenuous month. There have been many disappointments for which, in some respects, I apologize. In other respects, I Bless you for the growth you have achieved in your disappointments. What Christos said to you before is true. All your experiences shall lead you to your total integration and complete oneness within yourself.

Do not think that Spirit delights in seeing you experiencing disappointment, aggravation and hurt. Know that all that is done is truly done in Light and Love for your best interests, for your growth as well as your protection. Each of you shall have within you a mind of steel and a will of iron. This is necessary, for when you embark upon your mission to serve our Divine Father the road shall not be a bed of roses but shall be full of obstacles: hatred manifested to you, jealousy, and many other things that will require you to be of steel in order to accomplish your goals.

Allow your Masters to teach you in their way. Learn and understand the reasons for every action they take. I am going to relate an experience we were involved with last week to give you some sort of example as to what faces you, when you will set out on your path.

We were asked to lecture in another city last week. The subject was "The evolution from psychic to spiritual healing." There were thirty people in attendance, more than half of whom have been actively involved in healing for many years. When the lecture was completed, there was not one person in the room who had ever related their healing abilities to spiritual purposes before. All were amazed at our philosophy: pleased, but amazed. It was indeed a case of the blind leading the blind. If among those who supposedly are evolved, we find them with their eyes closed, what are we to expect when we speak to the average man walking as yet unaware?

The task that is ahead for all the Children of Light may seem on, as well as underneath the surface, impossible to achieve. Yet it shall be done. The devotion and dedication that is being manifested here, as well as in the multitudes of other Circles of Light surely shall prevail. Realize that one must lend support to the other. Broaden the scopes of your vision. Open your minds to the problems that your brothers and sisters present to you. Lend your services and your time and knowledge to ensure that others can survive on their own path, for all truly are as one.

This is the message I bring you tonight. I now turn this portion of the meeting over to Michael, and I Bless you in our Divine Father's Name.

Michael: Planetary physical Changes

Bless you. This is Michael.

We are going to talk tonight about the physical changes that will occur in the United States within the next twenty years. Understand that the changes we will discuss have a variable quality depending upon the progress that is made up to that point in raising the vibrations on this planet. The changes truly shall occur. The most significant change that will occur, and the one I am sure is most familiar within your minds, relates to what is known as the St. Andreas Fault. This rift within the bowels of the Earth may, within six or seven years, effect a splitting off of the land mass on the western side of the fault.

This will create a channel approximately two hundred and fifty miles wide. It will run from the southern part of California curving up, narrowing, and ending at a point in northern Nebraska.

I wish to ease your minds in relation to the population that is now residing in the areas to be affected by the split. It shall not be that sudden. There shall be tremors of a high enough magnitude to concern the scientists and the people residing there. I wish you to understand that this is not to punish anyone or destroy anyone. It is part of a cyclic cleansing and change that the planet must go through at that time.

On the eastern part of the United States, the Mississippi River shall become an ocean way approximately two hundred miles wide. This will form a land mass between the St. Andreas Fault on the west and the Mississippi River on the east in the shape of a pyramid. It will, for all practical purposes, divide the existing continental United States into three separate sections and land masses.

There shall be on all coastal areas, devastation, and flooding. Once again, not to punish and destroy, only as a result of the shifting of the land masses against the pressures of the oceans.

The triangle of land shall indeed be a spiritual mass, for it shall draw to it a concentration of God's Energies. Within this changing in the Earth mass, many of the tunnels beneath the surface of the Earth shall be destroyed, and many shall be uncovered. This will open to all new areas of exploration and enlightenment.

The state of Florida will be totally submerged in water for a period of three to five years. At that time, it shall rise again, and with it shall appear an elevation of Atlantis.

There shall indeed be other Earth changes within the structure of North America, limited shifting of land and water, but it shall not create massive havoc and destruction. There will be no need, as some Children are doing at this time, to prepare underground shelters or areas of survival for themselves, their families and associates. Some are stocking these shelters with rations, and also equipping them with an arsenal of weapons to defend themselves against their brothers who may wish to seek shelter. This type of action is abominable, for a true Child of Light knows that if it is his Father's Will for him to survive and continue his work, he shall. He shall be directed to an area of safety and shall have faith in his Father without concern.

I ask you all to take the words I have spoken to you, place them in your memory banks, and leave them there for the time being. Bless your Father when you awake every morning for another day of life. Live that day in love and growth, knowing in your heart that He shall provide for you. This is our only concern. All the rest shall come to pass as it is supposed to be.

Now it is time for me to turn the rest of the session over to someone who is waiting to speak to you. I Bless you for sharing your energies with Me this night.

God Bless you.

The Spirit of Christ: The Destiny of Man

God Bless you. I speak to you with the energies of the Spirit of Christ to bring to you a few sentences to perhaps further your understanding in relation to your position in the future destiny of man.

Nevermore shall my energies be incarnated totally as one to walk this plane. The Second Coming has already begun, but it is taking place in tens of thousands of Children of Light who have been, and who shall be touched by the pure Light. They are to live in the vibration of pure Love, to draw to them the unaware souls walking the face of the Earth. Only in this manner shall the world truly achieve spiritual oneness. It has truly been realized that many are needed to accomplish this work, and so it has been done.

I Bless you in our Divine Father's Name.

Sananda: Questions and Answers

This is Sananda.

It is time for the questioning period. James will please act as monitor.

Question to Michael: It appears that a shifting in the Earth of such a great magnitude would affect building construction and possibly natural entities as well. Is that going to happen in a great magnitude?

Answer: Within certain areas it shall occur as you have spoken. On an overall basis, it shall not be so. There are certain areas that shall incur great devastation. It is hoped that enough warning shall be given early enough so that the devastation shall not involve great loss of life.

Question to Michael: What relation, if any, does the Book of Revelations have to what you are saying?

Answer: It ties in closely with our words. The only thing we can say to you is when a book is read with a certain amount of knowledge within the mind, the resulting interpretation of the book comes along one path. When this book is re-read with additional information, or a grown scope of understanding, the book takes on a different meaning. It is read with a different set of eyes, a different awareness in the same individual. Re-read the book.

Question to Murvin: Why is it that someone looking through a telescope does not notice that it is not a planet, a star, but a ship?

Answer: The explanation is quite simple. Scientists have decided that Jupiter I, in its position around the Earth, is a star that is radiating off gases that shoot out colors.

whose aura is gases. They have accepted this as fact and leave us alone.

Question to Murvin: What star do the scientists call the Jupiter I?

Answer: I believe it is called, strangely enough, Dogs Head.

Question to Murvin: My friend has pulled through thirty symbols along with the vibration tones that go with them. Are these all from the Jupiter I?

Answer: No. They are not all from Jupiter I. If you will be patient for a moment, we shall tell you of their exact origin. He is pulling them from the planet Venus.

Question to Murvin: Can the symbols be used for healing?

Answer: Most assuredly.

Question to Sananda: Recently I have been having a lot of trouble with a brother in Santa Fe. He heads a school in natural healing. He is not acting as one would expect someone in his position to act. I need someone to help me handle this situation.

Answer: Each of us serves a specific function. On occasion, a teacher shall appear and begin to teach, to teach others that he does not know how to teach, to teach others in the form of a test to use their own minds and discern their own truth, not to sit and look upon him or her as a guru and absorb every word they say as total truth. There are some who are capable of relating to this man and use the knowledge in a positive fashion. You fall in the category of those who do not and never shall. We would suggest that you sever the relationship but learn from it. Then the association shall have been a positive one.

Question to Sananda: May I ask if the song, "My Ivory Tower", is not the vibrations that the Creator has sent through a particular person to show the Love that He has for mankind?

Answer: Most musical vibrations that are manifested in songs and words truly emanate from Spirit. As you all know, a musical note is indeed a vibration of spiritual energy and has great power and ability to soothe as well as to heal, to teach as well as to listen. The song will have healing effects on some and not on others. It depends on the vibrations of the person hearing the music.

Question to Murvin: About two weeks ago a friend of mine was engaged in attempting to integrate. During the course of this integration, she called upon you for aid. I will give you a visualization of this person, and I would like to know if you confirm that it was indeed yourself that came to her.

Answer: The answer is, of course, yes.

Question to Murvin: Early last Monday I received a message that a ship had landed. I was given a picture of a mountain off center, near a waterfall at the base. I assumed that the ship was supposed to be there. Can you enlighten me on this?

Answer: We could confirm this for you and enlighten you further. However, I am sorry, but I shall not do so. The further confirmation for this you shall have to obtain from within. Do it this way rather than to use me as an easy answer for yourself. We wish this answer to be difficult for you. I do not say that to you as a joke. I say this to you to assist you in obtaining your own truth from within.

Question to Sananda: Can you release the information on what ships will be used to pick up the Light Workers for detoxification?

Answer: It has been stated previously that the first ascension will be made by a limited group. When this has been completed, then plans for a larger group to be taken aboard for detoxification will be affirmed. Those who will make the first ascent shall be told 36 hours before the ascent. No one will be told who else is ascending with them. Each one must have faith in their own mission. For this reason, I cannot reveal any more information.

Before we close the session for tonight, I ask all to sit in a position of meditation. We shall once again this week expose you to one of the higher rays of Evangeline. Tonight, we expose you to the ray of French Blue banded in gold. Use it whenever you begin a lecture or speech by sending it to the audience. It shall raise their spiritual vibrations and increase their receptivity when you speak to them of God's Truth.

And now I call tonight's session to a close in the Name of our Divine Father. Bless us all.

Chapter 4

Newahjac: Planet Earth

I am the energies of Newahjac.

I have been summoned by our Divine Father to speak to you this evening and have received permission from Christos to use him for this purpose. I have spoken in this house before several years ago, but the time was not proper for those to hear the words I am here to speak. I am very old and ancient. I reside in the highest hierarchy. These are the first words I have spoken to more than one soul at a time in several thousand years.

We begin tonight with the creation of the planet Earth. This planet was created almost 74 billion years ago. It was not the size that it is today. It was indeed four and a half times larger than it is at this time. Various forms of deterioration and interplanetary collisions have reduced this planet to its present size. Its orbital path and revolutionary movements have effected substantial surface changes to reshape this planet to a globe after parts of it were either destroyed or broken away.

The planet Earth is undergoing an alteration in its orbital path. There will be a realignment of the planets within this Solar System. This will be done to save the planet Earth from destruction. It will use gravitational pull to help the planet retain its path of orbit within this Solar System.

This planet was created with a very specific purpose for its inhabitants in mind, to create the type and variety of physical atmosphere and conditions necessary to allow the incarnated soul to achieve a level of growth within the karmic pattern of development in certain specific areas.

The Plan has not always been as productive as we here would like it to be. Too large a percentage of mankind lock themselves into the emotional vibration reaction and forget to realize that they have a spiritual obligation to rise above this level and seek their Oneness with their Father.

This is your overall mission, not only you, but all those Children of Light that sit in thousands of other circles throughout this globe. This is all I bring you this night. Let us call it a mutual introduction of vibrations: yours to mine, and mine to yours. May our Father Bless us all.

Sananda

Good evening my brothers and sisters. This is Sananda.

We are going to change the format for tonight's program at this time. We are going to dispense with a lecture and the normal area of questions and answers. Instead, we are going to circle the room and bring each of you a message to perhaps enlighten you and ascertain for you a short and long-range mission along your spiritual path.

We advise and request that each of you listen intently to all the words spoken to the others. Most messages are rarely given for one, but for all. We may begin now, starting on My right.

Lanita: We Bless you, Lanita. You shall begin your final initiation within a period of seven weeks. Your mission shall be in the area of healing the emotionally disturbed, and of pictorial, spiritual art. The latter, I am sure, already has begun to manifest itself. The beauty and deep meanings within your work shall relate many stories, and bring much beauty and love to many, many people.

Blossom: We Bless you, Blossom. You are in the last stages of your final initiation.

It shall come to fulfillment before the summer of 1979. Your mission is to be a mother, a mother to God's Children of Light, not to counsel those who cannot counsel themselves, but to counsel those who can.

Ann: We Bless you, Ann. You have undergone three specific energy changes in your body during the past several months. The travels you have just returned from have brought you to areas necessary for you to visit. They have exposed you to the energies from these locations to help recall the ancient vibrations within your soul and will enable you to raise your conscious vibrations. Your mission shall be one of uniting. Your mind and strength shall be an important factor to those who are too busy to concern themselves with details, and who lack the drive to do the things that must be done.

This is primarily the reason that you have experienced the trials and suffering in your life, to build this strength. In addition, we say to you that before the first of the year you shall achieve spiritual communication at the conscious level.

Julie: We Bless you, Julie. You are a Child of Love, born of a vibration of love to draw yourself to those who are in need and who are troubled, to teach them to begin to understand what love is all about. This may seem like a simple path to you, but perhaps it is the most important path one may have. It is the greatest lesson that all mankind must learn.

Emogene: We Bless you, Emogene. We are dear friends, for we have chatted many times before. Basically, your path is known to you, but we shall embellish it at this time. There shall be a new area of involvement revealing itself to you in the area of musical tones relating to musical vibrations. It will be a new challenge for you and will manifest much knowledge to you for you to share with your brothers and sisters.

Dwight: We Bless you, Dwight. Your path is to serve as an information center to assist others in their work and their growth, an information center in several areas serving as a channel for Spirit for those who come to you with questions, to have the capacity to answer their questions. Those who come to you lost will be directed where they may find a spiritual home, a brother or sister. You have the capacity within your vibrations to channel extreme Divine Truth to be shared with all.

Dianna: We Bless you, Dianna. The suffering shall soon end. The mission and the path shall not change. All that has ever been related to you that seems to be lies shall be truth. Your mission is wherever you need to be at any given time. For indeed, you are Dianna.

Judith: We Bless you, Judith. We will discuss a short- range mission with you. You are to seek of yourself the true Judith that is awaiting you, to learn who she is and to love her, to accept her and to share her with the world, to let the rest of the world love her. When this has come to pass, you shall embark on your mission for God.

Richard: We Bless you, Richard. Your mission is within your mind, and yet you do not see it. Your service to mankind is within your hands, and yet you do not allow it to make its appearance. We ask you to accept all that has been given to you with love as a beginning of your growth, not as a culmination of your growth. Seek with a passion to expand all areas of knowledge that you now possess and the abilities that you have at your command. Call upon the higher energies to flow through you. Then things shall flow to you that you cannot even dream of, and your mission shall be in front of your eyes.

Mary: We Bless you, Mary. You are a child whose eyes have opened, and we welcome you into God's Light. You shall in the course of the next several years be involved in counseling dealing with personality adjustments within society. Your spiritual growth and expanded awareness shall help you serve within this area for the next several years. At that point your life shall take a sharp turn, and new levels of energy shall manifest themselves to you. They shall greatly alter your life in a totally new direction.

Lois: Bless you, Lois. You are indeed an old and wise soul. Your mission is to be a rock, a pillar of strength for those you love to lean on. You have the facility of being there when the need arises for you to be there: a coordinator, one who ties it all together.

Linda: We Bless you, Linda. When you begin to realize that you are one of God's "favorite children", as are all His Children, and accept this fact in your mind, you shall stop playing games with your life. Then you shall express yourself in the directions for which you are here. You have come to this planet for a specific purpose. You shall not achieve this purpose until you make up your mind, consciously, that this is the path you wish to follow. When you have decided, then I shall come to you and tell you your mission.

Nona: We Bless you, Nona. You are here to teach. You are here to help someone take the pieces of their puzzle of life and fit them together, to use the various sciences, specifically astrology and numerology and perhaps the tarot, to help one unite one's vibrations into a solid pattern for one's life. In a period of five years your mission shall change, for you shall also become involved in the science of astronomy and a wider span shall be opened to you at that time.

Betty: We Bless you, Betty. You are indeed an ancient soul. To throw a little levity into the conversation, I see the time when we were gypsies together, My child. You have the ability within your vibrations to mesmerize others with your words, to speak to people and have them react to you as if they know in their hearts that the words you speak to them are truth. This is the character of your vibrations, and it shall grow in time, adding a dimension of confidence that will be reflected to others. You shall do extensive lecturing and shall be involved greatly in the area of mind control.

Paul: Bless you, Paul. Part of your development and growth is to serve in assisting others to achieve the end results of their missions, to serve as a John or a Peter, so to speak, to be the equalizer, the man of peace, the tower of strength. This role, in effect, will serve as a facet of your own initiation. It shall give you untold strength and wisdom to be used later in your mission of peace. You are here and now labeled a Child of Peace: the peacemaker.

Fay: Bless you, Fay. Yours is a vibration and a mission of service. Your vibrations are truly becoming one with Paul's, for even the peacemaker needs strength, love and wisdom.

Minna: We Bless you, Minna. You sit before us a victim of frustration, most of it unearned, and yet it exists. Your path is to share your vast knowledge and information, to become a center within yourself for others to seek out, to set yourself as a clearing house, to guide, to steer, to encourage others along their path of growth. You are as a lighthouse, Minna.

James: We Bless you, James. You are our Peter, and the time shall come when you shall venture forth into the four corners of the Earth to speak God's Word to all who will hear.

Daria: We Bless you, Daria. All those who will not listen to your mate in peace shall listen to you in turbulence, for there are many who must be shaken, and then fondled with love, two talents you use so well. Your path shall be as your husband's, and the vibrations of oneness shall become stronger as the years pass by.

Wolfgang: We Bless you, Wolfgang. You who have suffered so much, the sun is about to rise on the horizon. Your enduring faith and devotion shall soon bear fruit. The time is drawing near for you to depart and begin your project, your mission. When the journey is made, an eternal beam of love and strength shall go with you to light your path, day and night.

Ron: We Bless you, Ron. There is not too much for me to say to you that you are not already aware of: however, I will make a comparison to one who rides the horse on the merry-go-round. His arms are three feet longer than those of the average child, and yet he refuses to pluck the brass ring.

Carmen: We Bless you, Carmen. Your mission is in your hands. You are to heal, to soothe, for your fingers contain magic and the energy shall continue to grow and serve you well.

Adrian: We Bless you, Adrian. You too shall serve in a capacity of organization and administration. The levels of your spiritual growth shall continue to grow and expand in many areas. Your mission shall always involve others, to be their strength and their rock.

Alan: We Bless you, Alan. We realize that you are having a most difficult time adjusting to this planet. Your mission is, of course, science, to rediscover many so-called inventions, methods of producing energy, and so on, that mankind refuses to acknowledge. Have patience, forge ahead with your work, and your day shall truly come.

DeLayne: We Bless you, DeLayne. Your mission shall involve relaying information and education obtained from our brothers in space. You shall decipher codes and languages to be shared with others, and to bring them new applications and uses of energies.

Sandy: We Bless you, Sandy. Your path is blossoming for you like a rose. You have accepted all others as they are and bless them. You have much to write and much to share. Your counseling and your teaching shall decrease as time passes, and your lecturing and writing shall increase. You are one of those who are to reach the masses, not the few. You shall present new theories to stimulate the minds of those who come to listen to your words.

Stuart: We Bless you, Stuart. We wish to congratulate you on the progress you have made in your growth this past year. Your path shall lead you to affiliation with an existing structure of an organization which you shall eventually head. You shall serve as a leader and a coordinator in their spiritual affairs.

Janice: We Bless you, Janice. Your development is truly just beginning to unfold. There are levels of awareness and consciousness that shall come to you within the next nine months that shall change the course of your life. At that time, you shall be asked to make a decision that will affect the course of your life spiritually. Depending upon your decision will rest your spiritual mission.

Debi: We Bless you, Debi. Allow the love of yourself to flow from your heart into your conscious mind. Realize that you are the most important person to you, and then you shall have the capacity to share your love with mankind. Then the doors from God shall open and embrace you, and your path will be made known to you.

Randy: We Bless you, Randy. Once we get rid of the stubbornness, you shall be able to make great progress. You will learn many things from your space brothers. We advise you to spend as much time as possible meditating in the mountains to bring you closer to the spacial vibrations. This is where your true teaching and learning shall come from. You shall serve as an emissary.

Gail: We Bless you, Gail. Your mission is to love and be loved, to care for those who do not have the time to care for themselves, to organize and to coordinate, and most of all to protect so that our Father's Work will be done.

Before we close this session for this month, I want all of you to understand that for some of you the words may have come in the form of a riddle. For some, they may have seemed hard and cold. Know that all has come in love and truth. I do not sit here to judge or to be judged. I sit here to share, to learn and to teach, for we truly are as one. Accept your vibrations and your mission, and all shall become clearer and clearer. If there are any questions, we still have some time to answer them.

Question: A combination of humanitarian rose color and Christ metallic gold has been coming to me in dream state. Is this a source of energy available to all people on this planet, or is it for myself?

Answer: It is available for all those whose vibrations have reached the level capable of handling this ray. In theory it is here for all mankind to use when they are capable of compatibility with its vibrations and energy levels.

Question: What is the possibility, and is it a good idea to have a physical information center within the city?

Answer: It is an excellent idea. The opportunity for this shall arise in the next few months, for things shall start to fall into place rapidly now. There is a great need for such a facility.

Question: The organizations and other seeking groups within the valley, shall they be contacted to join the group of Light Workers regardless of who they are?

Answer: It does not matter what they call themselves. If they walk in God's Light, contact them. The label they place on themselves is of no importance.

We are going to call this session to a close at this time. May our Divine Father Bless us all in His Light and Love.

Chapter 5

Newahjac: Devastation on Planet Earth

These are the energies of Newahjac speaking to you. Bless you.

My heart is bursting with joy and pride to see this floor covered with so many Children of Light.

I come to you tonight to speak to you of love, love in relation to words many of you have heard concerning the devastation and destruction of the planet Earth. Each time so-called psychics speak words of destruction or chaos they are adding to the already building negativity surrounding this planet. So, I speak to you of love.

It matters not what changes take place within the structure of the surface of this planet. It matters not if continents rise or fall, for life is eternal. All that matters is universal brotherhood and love, to keep on a constant path of learning, seeking, sharing and learning again. I do not say that changes within the structure of this planet shall not occur, nor do I say that they shall. We who walk in the Light realize that the only constant we have is change, change for growth.

Do not run and build underground shelters and stock them with food, for that shall lead to stocking them with weapons. That shall lead to hate, not love. Run instead to our Father. Ask Him to teach you, to enlighten you, to help you reach the point within your growth enabling you to rise above all catastrophes. This is the way to prepare: to grow!

You have been told that there are 144,000 Children of Light consciously walking this planet. There are some 600,000,000 who have the capability of consciously realizing the Light. Seek and find them.

Do not hide in shelters. Embrace the world. That is my message for tonight, and I Bless you.

Michael: Energy Rays

This is Michael. Bless you.

It has been decided between the Spirit, Sananda and Myself that I shall have the honor of addressing you this evening. The ceiling of this room, in a spiritual sense, has already disappeared from the power of the vibrations that rise and rise. I am sure that all of you who sought out and brought with you another Child of Light this night feel a little larger flame within your hearts, a little more love within your being. That is as it should be, for it is part of your overall mission.

We are going to discuss the effects of certain remedies or extracts on the spiritual body, as well as certain levels of energy rays that are used in areas of spiritual healing.

There have been developed, many years ago, a series of extracts from flowers, trees, and other of nature's children, extracts known as the Bach Remedies. There will be many more such extracts dis-covered. Realize that from a scientific point-of-view, the process in-volved in making these extracts may seem to be very simple. It truly is not so. The process is a form of alchemic reaction. The belief in the Spirit, the belief in God's Children to heal must be present in order for the extracts to contain the spiritual "power" to heal the vibra-tions and the energy bodies of mankind.

We shall, in the future, assist in the area of correlating vibrations with each of the existing remedies. This may aid in the correct appli-cation of extract to illness to a finer degree. Imagine in your mind the beauty when one who is ill is lying in meditation listening to a musical vibration, bathed in a light of color that is a source of his Light, and touched with a drop that carries a healing vibration for his spiritual energies. For this too shall come to pass.

We have, through Our neglect, failed to copy the list of the higher rays of Evangeline for you at this session, for which We apologize. Let Me assure you that We shall prod him to do so for the next session. In any event, We shall relate to you at this time the beginning of the higher rays.

The thirteen basic rays have been established. The fourteenth ray is a ray of jet black, as if it were a shield of lead, a ray of protection to avoid exposure to all whose vibrations have not yet reached that level where they are capable of handling the rays from the fifteenth to the twenty-second level.

When a Child awakens and sees the Light, the ray of Fuchsia banded in silver shall appear from over the top of the black ray. It will make itself available to him to use in his work. Before five months have passed, I expect all of you to be at the levels where you shall have available to you these higher rays. While they are rays of service, of healing and communication without distortion or interference, their primary function is as follows: to enable you to walk the path emitting God's Vibrations to all you come in contact with, that when you meet a brother or sister, they shall instantly know that you walk in the Light, Truth and Love.

I must make you aware of one thing. Your vibrations shall grow to the intensity that those who do not walk in the Light may become uncomfortable in your presence. They will not be able to understand the power of the vibrations emanating from your being. Know and recognize this fact.

We shall introduce to you at next month's session several new methods of healing using certain types of arm and hand configurations to pinpoint the flow of energy. For this reason, we request that for next month's session you do not partake of any alcoholic beverages for at least twenty-four hours before the session.

There has been much movement and action within the heavens around this planet, and we are sure there are many questions to be answered this night.

Questions and Answers

We take your leave, and once again ask James to act as monitor. You may also call upon the energies of Murvin to answer some of your questions.

I Bless you all.

Question to Murvin: Last night I was watching television, and several low, bright lights appeared. I wondered if they were stars or something else. One of them was very colorful. They were in the east.

Answer: The three were not ships. The configurations and colors manifested due to atmospheric and weather conditions.

Question to Murvin: A few weeks ago, several of us were at Tonopah, and we were looking for a ship. We saw what we thought were ships, but we were not sure. They seemed to be in the configuration of a cross. We were facing east. Can you elaborate on this?

Answer: They too were not ships, but stars.

Question to Murvin: Some of us saw the picture on television by the media with the "Dove" in front of the moon. Their explanation was that Venus was eclipsed by the moon. Please verify.

Answer: The ship, the "Dove", was indeed in front of the moon.

Question to Murvin: There has been a mass exodus of ships leaving this area. Can you explain this?

Answer: There has not been a mass exodus of ships leaving this area. Some have withdrawn leaving greater distances between themselves and this planet for specific reasons. Some have moved as part of normal procedure to cover other areas for a while. This area is still quite adequately protected and serviced.

Question to Murvin: The sightings in Australia, New Zealand and other parts of the world: the increased visibility of these sighting and communication by the news media giving out this information, is this part of the program to show man?

Answer: It is indeed. The ships that were sighted were part of a Uranian task force consisting of ships #47, #72, #93, #114 and #137. This procedure shall not be what you refer to as a "flash in the pan". It shall be steady and increase in frequency as time passes.

Question to Murvin: Will the ships over the U.S. be shielded in their presence, or will they encourage acknowledgements of their presence?

Answer: When those who rule in the government of this country overcome their own fears and insecurities, when they work their way through the myriads of paperwork and tape to formulate a plan for releasing the validity of your space brothers, it shall be done as you have stated. However, we say to you that they shall be second in releasing this type of information. There shall be another government that shall declare the validity of your space brothers first. Then your government shall rush to acknowledge their presence.

Question to Sananda: Can we have more information in relation to Solomon's Temple and what role it is going to play in our growth?

Answer: The construction of Solomon's Temple has already begun in spiritual energy. A prospective site for the construction of the Temple has already been visited by Christos.

The function for the Temple shall be as follows: It shall indeed serve as a Center of Light for twelve Centers of Light to be established throughout this country. Its main function shall be similar to that of the Great Healing Temple of Atlantis, to heal the mind and the spirit, to teach man how to grow and to find God. Its vibrations shall make this location one of the great spiritual centers on Earth.

Question to Sananda: They have started setting up a learning exchange similar to one in Chicago. Will it be best to associate with a temple as you described, or start in a separate location?

Answer: We would suggest to you, for the time being, to begin to exert your energies toward a separate location. We do not wish you to waste time. Assimilation may occur later on. Start the energies flowing as soon as possible.

Question to Sananda: What has happened to Sister Melissa? What is she engaged in right now?

Answer: Sister Melissa is engaged in setting up new levels and regulations for a new spiritual council of advisement that is to be established in the next forty or fifty centuries.

Question to Sananda: There has been an epidemic of the "Russian flu" and other viruses. I understand that in some cases advantage has been taken for cleansing purposes. Can you clarify this for those that have undergone these cleansings and have not been able to heal themselves?

Answer: Quite true. The flu is a reality, and we might as well avail ourselves of the time and situation. There are many who have had, in addition to the flu, a period of cleansing. Many of those have experienced tightness and pain within certain areas of the lower back and the legs. This is partially due to changing levels of energy and reacclimation to the new level of vibrations in their bodies.

Question to Sananda: Could you expound on the being, Sanat Kumara, and his present position in the Hierarchy? Is he still with us, helping us? What is his relationship to you and the rest of the Hierarchy?

Answer: You have posed Me quite a complex question. Let Me search for a moment for the proper words so I will not place Myself in hot water. He is indeed a Child of God at the 12th station, meaning he is the 12th Child of God. His vibrations are indeed as Mine, as are Dianna's and many others. There could be a tendency to confuse one with the other. He is here as I am here. He is not here but everywhere, and always shall be, for this is his position.

Question to Murvin: Back in May we saw a series of lights on a mountainside in a horizontal position. We believed they were ships. We returned several weeks later, and they were gone.

Answer: There are very few ships whose locations are stable. Most of them do move and shift their locations from time to time. Only the command ships are fixed within a general location and remain there for long periods of time. Such is the case with the sighting that you experienced.

Question to Murvin: There was also some other activity further down the road, huge vehicles such as trucks. I felt that I should not go near the area and stayed clear. We returned the next day and there was no evidence of anything unusual.

Answer: I do not pick up anything out of the ordinary in the vibrations as you describe them. It could have just been the sensitivity within you at that time. I find no other answer for you.

Question to Murvin: I would like to share with my fellow man the understanding I have of heavenly bodies that can move in space. The reason for the appearance of the Dove before the Moon is that sometimes the Moon does move its position. Is this correct?

Answer: You are indeed correct.

Question to Murvin: Recently a brother of ours gave us some information that a certain number of ships were in the hands of our government. Were those ships intentionally allowed to be captured? Were any of them from the negative brotherhood operating in this sphere, or any other information you can give us on this topic?

Answer: Two of the vehicles were intentionally allowed to be captured. One ship, containing several lifeless forms.

was the result of an accident. None of them were of the negative brotherhood.

Question to Murvin: Since we are on this subject, perhaps we can share some more information on the matter. In 1954 the appearance of a Martian ship at Edwards Air Force Base in California occurred when our President was supposed to be present. Can you verify this?

Answer: That was quite a well-kept secret, and in fact, did occur.

Question to Sananda: At what point will the government release the information about the space brothers above the United States?

Answer: It is most difficult for Us to relate a specific time, as We are dealing with the free will of man. However, within a general area We can estimate eight or nine months.

Question to Sananda: In dealing with various channels, whether they be Sister Melissa, the Ruby Focus, or other various channels, what are the conditions and limitations that cause a difference in syntax and alteration of voice level and expression?

Answer: The soul of Christos has three facets: the energies of Sananda, Michael, and the Spirit. Each one of these energies' functions at a slightly different vibrational level. This causes a different voice quality and texture, resulting in a changing of expression in each case. All communication is coming to you from the soul. There is no longer any exterior channel permitted to come through directly.

Question to Sananda: Could we take Jane Roberts as an example of an external channel, or is she channeled information from her higher self?

Answer: She does indeed channel from the Hierarchy. The true name of the Spirit is Rulatin.

Question to Sananda: You say there will be a temple in this country. Will there be other temples in the world?

Answer: There will be many Centers of Light throughout the world. There shall be many twelves, and many twelve of twelve until the world becomes one, under God.

I speak to you in words and terms to answer many of the questions you have posed to Me that indicate that there shall be no devastation or destruction. A center shall rise in many of the areas that seem earmarked for destruction. Yet, I say to you, I do not deny nor confirm this destruction. The energies of Light that flow must continue to flow in a constant state, ever rising in a higher vibration. This is how you must lead your lives, to hear the information and the words of those who speak to you, to store it to use if these vibrations come to pass. In the meantime, continue to grow and love.

We Bless you all.

Chapter 6

Evangeline and the Color-Rays

Before we begin tonight's session, we shall talk consciously to you for a while. On the way home from the Ruby Focus last fall I was channeled the fourteenth through the twenty-second rays of Evangeline. There are thirty-six rays in all at this time that shall be available for use by mankind.

Some of you have been seeing color in your meditations. The time will come, or has come, when you will have a block in your meditation. You will have lost the color and all you will see is black. Nothing has happened, nor is anything wrong. You are being exposed to the fourteenth ray of Evangeline. This ray is a protective ray of black to protect mankind from the higher rays until their vibrations are able to handle these rays. Otherwise, the energy from these rays would have a destructive effect.

When the time comes that you yourself have raised your vibrations to the level where you can handle these rays, the fifteenth ray of Fuchsia banded in silver, will come to you in meditation and begin to rise over the black belt for your use.

All these colors from the fifteenth to the twenty-second rays are banded and contained, alternatingly, in silver and gold. The purpose for the banding is to prevent diffusion and distortion of these energies and vibrations. The rays are absolutely true, undistorted channels from the Source. They are channels of communication without any unnecessary adjectives or flowery words. Now is the time when we need only truth in everyday language. We need to know what is happening. We are not to sit in awe and not understand. We are to hear words that we can understand and absorb.

Some of the rays are for healing, some for communication with Masters, and some for-interspace communication. The last ray, the twenty-second, is of pearlized white banded in gold. It is the channel of communication with our Divine Father.

I am going to show you some new configurations of healing with the hands that have been given to me for use with these rays. We all know that there are seven basic chakras in the body. There are, of course, many more. We heal, at present, through eighteen. Most of them are located on the back. They are spiritual chakras and use energies at higher levels.

Insert the thumb between the second and third finger on each hand creating a pyramid on its side. Place one hand on each side of the area to be healed.

Interlock your thumbs with the thumbs of the person you are healing. Send energy with both hands. This will achieve a balancing between the physical and spiritual energies in the body.

Touch the second and fourth fingers of your hands with the second and fourth fingers of the other person. This is used to activate the pineal gland.

Touch the third and pinky finger of your hands with the third and pinky fingers of the other person. This will activate the pituitary gland and stimulate it.

Interlock your fingers in a crossed hand position with the other person's hands. This is used to reverse the field of energy polarity in the body.

Cup your fingers together and point them at the front and back of the head at the third eye. This will aid in raising vibrations.

Do not use any of these configurations for more than two minutes at a time, as they evoke a powerful flow of energy. These hand manipulations are primarily used to heal spiritual vibrations.

Now if you will be patient for a few moments, we shall begin.

Michael: The higher Rays of Evangeline

This is Michael. Bless you.

The energies of Newahjac will not be with us tonight, as some of our time has been spent discussing the Rays of Evangeline.

There has been an alteration in the setup of the energies in the soul of Christos due to the nature of conditions prevailing throughout the world. We will use the energies of Sananda for counseling, for teaching, and for all matters that require the softness of a woman's touch. I, Michael, shall be here to speak to you in strength and in force, when necessary, to give you the courage and the fortitude necessary for you to have in order for you to accomplish your missions. All of Us are, as always, available to you for any questions you may have to pose to us. We are pleased, and we Bless all the new Children of Light sitting within the circle tonight.

The vibrations of spiritual unity are spreading rapidly throughout your city. Each of you carries within your conscious mind the thought at all times to seek out and find another Child of Light. I am sure by now that some of you realize that by carrying this thought within your minds you are constantly elevating your own vibrations and enhancing your growth.

We wish to talk to you tonight on the proper usage, control and presentation of the higher Rays of Evangeline. These are not ordinary rays of light or energy. They have a vibration so sensitive that at times it is difficult to detect their presence. You will notice that most of the colors are in the pastel family. Some of them are combinations or blends of two separate hues.

When you have determined that you wish to use one of the rays for communication, healing or any other purpose in which they may assist you, it is your privilege to call upon Evangeline to release that specific ray to you for your purpose.

I must impress upon you the importance of not misusing these rays. To misuse them once will lose them to you for the balance of your life. Treasure them dearly. They are a gift from our Divine Father. Begin to allow them to flow through you using your third eye as an entry point into the physical vehicle. They will help you in raising the levels of your vibrations and conscious spiritual growth.

When you meet a brother or sister who, in your opinion, has reached a level of development where they are capable of handling and utilizing these rays, share them, for that is their purpose.

The 23rd to 36th rays shall be a reality for many of you during your lifetimes. They are rays that basically do not relate to this planet, its life and survival. They are rays of interplanetary communication, inter-ship communication of energy, dematerialized travel and higher thought transmission.

When you have reached the point within your development that you have been totally cleansed, detoxified, and have become one within yourself, then you shall be individually instructed in the proper usage of some of these rays. It will depend upon your mission and which area you are to serve in.

I urge you, one and all, to set up a stable program for daily meditations. I hear some of you saying to yourselves, "some days I just cannot find the time." There is always time for God, for He always has time for you. I would say that He is a little busier than you are. Meditation for you is no longer a reason for relaxing the body and mind. It has become a potent tool for you to use to enhance your growth and knowledge. It is a time of study, of learning and assimilation. It is a necessity for your growth and development.

There are the words I share with you this night, for Sananda wishes to speak. I Bless you, My brothers and sisters.

Sananda: The difference between love and hate

This is Sananda speaking. Bless you.

It is a pleasure to feel the vibrations of love and warmth within this Circle of Light. I am here to talk to you of love, of the differentiation between love and hate, understanding and judging. We have had imposed upon us during the course of this past month several judgment decisions. I must say to you that We allowed this to affect Our vibrations and for negativity to enter Our sphere of influence.

There are many of God's Children who walk their path with blinders. They allow into their vision and into their mind's areas of truth with which they can relate and assimilate within this limited scope. When they fall upon one who's ideas or philosophy varies from their own, their ego forces them to reject this, casting negative vibrations on another soul. This has happened to us, and in truth, it can happen to all of you. Do not react in anger or hate. React in love. We took firm action within the situation. However, with the firmness was love and healing energies. For if not, then we too would be guilty of judging another soul. The line is thin. Many times, rebuttal can be in the form of return judgment instead of being in the form of a lesson, of seeking to have the other understand your truth and allowing you to express it freely.

The soul who walks in ego, or who walks without the capacity for acceptance of his sister or brother will most assuredly learn the lesson within the current lifetime. This is not the category or nature of karma that is delayed to another incarnation. Send love and your blessings, and it shall help that particular soul overcome his limited outlook, and in his growth.

These are the words I share with you tonight. If you will all take a few moments and sit in a position of meditation, the Spirit is going to activate your third eyes to enable you to utilize the higher rays of Evangeline.

I Bless you. My brothers and sisters.

Questions and Answers

Now it is time for the questioning period. James shall act as monitor. The energies of Murvin shall also be available for your questions.

Question to Michael: I have an impression to correct channeling in a certain direction. We are coming into the time of high energies, and I wish to clarify a question which is of importance to us all. Today the New Age is using hypnosis and misusing the channeling of energies through that word. I would like clarification that hypnosis and our understanding, going back to Atlantis, does or does not mean separation of consciousness from being. If that is so, then hypnosis is the usage of black magic and false energy. Trance is permissible channeling. Awareness is the highest form of channeling. I feel that hypnotism is interfering with the individual choice by separating consciousness from being. Is this correct?

Answer: We shall have to qualify Our answer for you. In the level of hypnotic state that we call an altered state of consciousness or deep meditation, there is truly no harm created. When we are delving into deep hypnotic trance the information can be true or false, depending on the questions and suggestions that the administrator is planting within the questions. If the one directing the hypnotic state is not allowing or picking up the vibrations of the subject properly, he can steer the answers to the desired direction.

We do not wish to be so harsh as to say it is black magic, for we must allow freedom of expression. However, we would say to you that due to the levels of the basic vibrations of most of God's Children on this planet, the deep hypnotic level is not desirable or necessary. To achieve knowledge of past lives or past experiences, we can accomplish this totally on the conscious level in a deep meditative state.

We believe that when the subject is conscious, he will truly learn from the vibrations of the past. He is able to feel, to rationalize, to understand. The experience will occur without being steered or controlled in a specific direction.

Question to Michael: I was not referring to misguiding as far as hypnotism goes. Rather the word hypnotism leads to that which we call black magic. When someone uses the privilege of consent from someone else and misuses energies by interfering with his consciousness, this is the area of danger.

Answer: In all areas we have those who would practice the black arts. We also have those who are legitimate. However, we would agree that it offers exposure and temptation to many things that are not desirable. If the information can be obtained by other methods, it would be far safer to use them.

Question to Sananda: In an open letter from the Rainbow Ray Focus, there was a channeling of Sananda referring to Light Workers entering a higher level for cleansing and detoxification. It says that it is the time not to eat dairy products, much less fish and meat. Does the individual have to determine whether he has reached this point, or was it a channeling for all Light Workers to do now?

Answer: The words I spoke were words with double meaning. For those whose minds follow my channeling to the letter without using their own free will, it was meant for them to do so immediately. For those who use their minds to discern, to discriminate, to pull out of the words of Spirit what relates to them in their truth, it becomes an individual matter based on one's needs and field of action.

In actuality, when the time comes for you to cease eating or drinking certain foods or liquids, your body shall inform you of this need. Your vibrations shall rise to the point where the vibrations of what you are taking into your system will have lost the compatibility. Do not feel that because you are a vegetarian, or because you eat fruit you are walking any closer to your Father. This is not always true.

Question to Michael: When a person is going through a long-term spiritual cleansing, it also manifests physically. I assume this is true. How can we hold up under the stresses that have physical effects?

Answer: In order not to combat but to aid in this cleansing and purification, and yet at the same time maintain some physical stability and normal life, it is necessary for you to work with the energies that have come to you. This can only be achieved by daily energizing and meditations. It is true that the cleansing puts a strain on the physical body. It requires constant energizing to maintain stability.

Some will say that when they are down with the flu, a fever, an ache or soreness that it is difficult for them to meditate. This may be true. However, these ailments will never interfere with a self-energizing program to restore your vibration levels to normal.

Question to Michael: I have been under some physical strain. I have received professional care and I seem to be worse. May I please have some advice to help my situation?

Answer: We would suggest to you that the time has come when your system is rejecting tobacco. We recommend a three-day liquid diet to cleanse your system of these vibrations. You should also make an affirmation relating to your good health indicating that you no longer smoke.

Question to Sananda: I was wondering if a person's spirits will help them maintain a vegetarian diet?

Answer: Living on a fruit and vegetarian diet will not insure one of spiritual growth. It is like calling God when one has a problem and wondering why he does not answer.

Spiritual growth is not a part-time project. It is an all- consuming existence. Eating the proper food without the rest is like water down the drain.

Question to Murvin: I have a strange problem with my being. Whatever it is, it saps my strength, and is quite painful. I don't know what to do for it. I have had it for a long time.

Answer: When you return home tonight, lie on your back with your hands at your sides, palms up. We shall astrally transport you aboard ship to balance and restore the flow of energy to your vibrations. It will be necessary for you to energize yourself daily to maintain the energizing we shall give you.

Question to Michael? Why is it that the work I do at night when I sleep tires me out? Can I do the work and not be tired when I wake?

Answer: Basically, it is a state of mind. While you are growing spiritually at night part of your mind is saying, "I should not be doing this for I shall be tired." Before you retire this night, let the last thought that passes through your mind be one that you accept the learning that shall come to you this night. You also accept the fact that it shall not tire you nor cause you lack of energy the next day.

Question to Murvin: How many alien souls are there in this room?

Answer: There are eleven, all told.

Question to Sananda: For the past two months things have been very difficult in my life. In the past few weeks, the stresses that would make my life more difficult have been removed. Is this an effect of astrological forces, or are there other forces involved?

Answer: Most assuredly, the astrological forces are affecting your life at this time. This energy flow can alter your life. However, there are other matters and factors to be considered. If you can, within your conscious mind begin to understand that all that flows to you is for a purpose, to face these situations as if you expect them to have arisen, to try to understand why they have arisen. Then rise over them and utilize them for your own advantages. Handle them with stable vibrations and maintain emotional and physical balance.

Question to the Spirit: What advice do you have for someone who has a fatal kidney disease, a hereditary disease that slowly, year by year, is destroying him. Medically there is no cure. Do you have any advice?

Answer: The individual soul must understand that although this disease is hereditary, it was their choice to incarnate into this condition. Try to understand the reason behind having the condition. See if in the mind the need is actual at this time, if it is truly necessary for them to learn from it. If it is no longer needed, then We recommend that the individual ask his Father to release the disease, as it will have served its purpose. Begin a nutritional program. Use energy healing, and faith in themselves and in our Father.

Question to Michael: About a week ago, I was lying on the couch and fell asleep. A face appeared. I believe it was a man's face. Can you tell me who this was?

Answer: It was a manifestation of one of your Masters beginning to establish communication with you by showing his presence. We suggest that you call upon one of the several Masters you have been given and see if you can solidify the contact. Do not ask us for the name. You already know our answer.

Question to Michael: The night before last, Faye and I were sleeping, and she was awakened during the night in a state of extreme fear. She detected two energies in the room and was driven by fear to attack the energies. During the course of this experience, she called upon me for help. I rose, uttered several sentences in a language she did not understand, but which reassured her, and seemed to stop the energies. Soon she went back to sleep. I would like to know what words I said, and what were those energies?

Answer: The child that she carries in her belly, who is about to enter your world, is a very special child. It is, even now, subjected to vibrations of negativity seeking to deter it from its path. This was the energy that manifested itself in her presence. The child is under very heavy protection. From time to time the negativity shall appear in an attempt to reach the child. The words you spoke were of ancient Aramaic. They basically stated that the child is under God's protection, walks in his Light, and shall always do so.

Question to Michael: I had a similar experience with my companion. She was very frightened. I was not asleep and wanted to say something or do something to calm her down. Three words came into my mind. They sounded to me like they were Latin. I have forgotten them and would like to know what they were.

Answer: The words were ancient Hebrew and are part of a phrase that offers a great positive protection. We shall repeat the phrase for all of you. "Kadosh, kadosh, kadosh. Adonoy tzvaos, milo chall ha aretz kivodo." In English it means, "Blessed, blessed, blessed is the Lord. The one Lord over all the earth." It is one of the most powerful mantras or blessings available to man.

Question to Sananda: Perhaps you can give me some guidance in releasing people from one's life, and why it is necessary to do so?

Answer: This answer pertains to you all. In the inter relationship between two people there is an exchange of vibrations for each to share, to love and to experience. When it comes to a point within the spiritual growth that this relationship of vibrations is no longer necessary, that the things to be learned have been learned, the flow of energy ceases. The two walk apart to seek another of a different vibration to learn and share with. When one has become emotionally involved with the vibration, one must transmute it in meditation and release it to enable one to walk in peace and love. All things, when done, must be sealed and finished with love. It will hamper your growth to allow energies tied into an old situation to remain. When it is done, it must be totally released. Then one may rise and walk ahead in life.

Question to Sananda: I have some trouble at times with a feeling of being apart or separate from people and the world. I would like some guidance in how to handle this and continue my growth.

Answer: When you will learn to love and accept yourself exactly as you are, then the trouble you have relating to others shall disappear. It shall no longer be important to you what they think or how they react to you. You shall have achieved self-love, self-understanding and awareness. You shall be able to walk in your truth and live it. Look at yourself: do not be afraid. Accept yourself and allow yourself to love you as you are.

Question to Sananda: Would it be good for me to experience rebirth?

Answer: A Child of God may begin a life span of some 80 years, and at the age of 79 and a half become aware of the presence of his soul.

He will, at that moment, fulfill the destiny of his incarnation. It does not matter when one becomes aware, only that it happens.

Chapter 7

Sananda: 1984 A.D.

Bless you My brothers and sisters. This is Sananda.

This will be the last session in which there shall be a separate and distinct vibration from Myself, Michael and the Spirit. This night the unity of oneness shall have been completed, and all the vibrations shall be as one. Next month We begin to call these sessions "An Evening with Christos."

We Bless all those Children who are gracing our Circle of Light for the first time and wish them continued success on their path toward self-realization.

The subject for tonight's session relates to the year 1984 A.D. This year is a master year, a twenty-second year. It will be the beginning and the introduction of a new basic level of vibrations on the planet Earth. This is what We wish to discuss with you and begin to introduce to you this night.

The solar eclipse that took place several days ago benefitted many greatly by permitting the assimilation of higher vibrations to flow through their being. Many of you seemed tired, listless and heavy. It was due to the assimilation of this energy bringing you to new levels of growth that are being made available to you at this time. You must understand that when the basic vibration begins to change the work that all of you shall face shall first begin.

They shall come to you by the multitudes. To you, and to circles like this throughout the world seeking, asking help, wishing to know what sort of changes are taking place within them. The vibrations of the Children of Light must, by necessity, be one level higher than the levels of vibrations of the planet in general. This will enable them to do their work properly and efficiently.

We are not going to discuss the physical Earth changes at this time. But, in a way, perhaps We must mention it briefly. There are those of God's Children walking this planet to whom raising the level of a vibration may increase a flow of negativity at the conscious level, for they walk in a negative expression. For this reason, it has become necessary, beginning now, for all the Children of Light to send love to all of their brothers and sisters throughout the world. Begin now to raise the vibrations of love to overcome the flow of negativity and avert destruction. Do this to avert chaos, not from an Earth physical point-of- view, but from a humanity point-of-view. Begin to ease the amount of negativity emanating from the face of this planet and transmute it to a vibration of love.

By the year 1990 A.D., all of the Children of Light shall be totally in-tegrated, living the role of total commitment, and fulfilling their ob-ligations to our Divine Father. Many of you have already begun to notice drastic changes within the physical and chemical structure of your bodies. More of you shall be aware of this in the future. Talk to one of your brothers and sisters. Ask them if they have had similar experiences. Interrelate with one another. Help each other to grow, to understand. In doing so you shall enhance your own growth.

The time for unity has never been stronger or more imperative. Re-alistically speaking, with all of your prayers and all of your Blessings of love, there shall still be chaos. There shall be danger and there shall be death. In the evolution of time changes occur when it is time for them to occur. Those who walk with our Divine Father shall con-tinue to do so, unafraid. They shall know in their hearts that all shall be well for them, for indeed, it shall. In the year 2,000 A.D. the spir-itual revolution that has already begun to occur, the second coming of the Messiah, which has already occurred in every child of God walking this planet, shall have taken a very strong foothold within the countries throughout this planet. If not, the civilization as it is known today shall be doomed. I do not say this to frighten you. Conversely, we say this to reassure you. For those who walk with their Father, fear not.

By the year 2,000 A.D. all the Children of Light shall be in total mental telepathic communication. They shall be able to heal a Child of God with merely a touch. Some of you will have learned and acquired the ability of energy dematerialization as a means of transporting yourselves. No longer is it necessary for one of you to ask the question, "How much longer must I wait before I find out what my mission is?" This is the overall plan.

These are the words I speak to you this night. Assimilate them slowly, and if they fit into your truth accept them in your hearts. Accept them and live them. I Bless all of you.

Michael: Spaceships for new vibrations

This is Michael, and I Bless you.

Now perhaps you will understand why I have spoken so sternly the past few sessions. It is not because I am the ogre. It is because I supply the strength and the fortitude. As each day passes, more and more of you shall feel My Energies present within your vibrations. As you reach the point within your level of growth when you are entitled to receive that portion of our Father's Energies that contain My Vibrations, you shall receive them. They will give you the courage and the strength to survive through your initiations and your periods of growth.

Long before the year 2,000 A.D. there shall be space landings on the planet Earth. Most of you shall, if not physically, assuredly astrally, be taken aboard ship for cleansing and detoxification. Before a new level of energy is made available to you the system must be cleansed and prepared for the entrance of the new vibration.

When in your meditation you are informed that you are to be taken aboard ship for cleansing, preface the journey with this statement: "I release myself to a ship of God in Light and Love." There are indeed negative fleets of ships. The more your vibrations rise, the more sensitive you become to the negativity, and the more powerfully you shall feel it. Be consistently aware of the necessity to protect your vibrations to insure that your aura remains sealed.

During the days ahead if you are troubled, if you are in a place within your growth that you need extra strength or reassurance, you may call upon Me for My Vibrations to supply your needs. It shall be my honor to do so. I do not know when I have enjoyed sharing as much as I have enjoyed sharing in this circle. Although my vibrations shall not come to you again totally as Michael, most assuredly they shall be here, and you shall always know My Words.

I charge you to fulfill your destinies for your Father, for each of you has chosen this incarnation to do so. Assume your role and your responsibilities.

May our Father Bless you all.

Questions and Answers

Now it is time for the period of questioning. James will act as monitor. Please commence.

Question to Michael: Around last Christmas time was there false information channeled from above, or was the information wrong? I have been requested to ask this question.

Answer: There are always sources that channel down misinformation. Christmas time was no exception. If you would be more specific as to the source and the recipient, perhaps We can give you a more concise answer.

("The channel who received for me received some information, and later on, information from someone on the other side that the first information was incorrect.")

That is quite true. The channel was in the process of learning a very important lesson. Unfortunately, you were the recipient of the misinformation, for the lesson was not yours.

Question to Michael: In Sedona there is a source who is doing cleansing work. We received information that there was a split situation above. Has that been clarified by now?

Answer: The split situation you are referring to has indeed been clarified. For the present, I can comment no further.

Question to Spirit: Some months back while meditating in this room, I had an experience similar to ones I had in childhood which frightened me very much. Would you please explain this?

Answer: You are indeed a Child of Light. Your vibrations are very soft, tender, and extremely sensitive. In all such instances when a Child of high vibrations is incarnated, the negative forces often seek to attack, to deter and dissuade the soul from completion of its path. Your spiritual vibrations lay dormant for many years. Upon their awakening this force once again manifested itself. However, we may say to you that it shall not happen to you again.

Question to anyone: I was told on Wednesday in one of my meditations that I was to be here this evening for a very special purpose, that I would be made aware of it as "Elambria". I would like clarification from anyone who would like to speak on this matter.

Answer: My dear beloved daughter. These are the energies of your Father speaking to you. My Voice, if it quavers, does so from the energy power. We have waited a long, long time for this moment. For indeed, the time has come for your total cleansing and unification to allow you to begin to release all vibrations within your physical presence that have tormented you for so many years. Your devotion to your Father, and to all those who seek you out is at last complete beyond all doubts. I take this moment within the presence of your brothers and sisters to give you a final baptism of love to elevate your vibrations to those of total oneness and purity, to grant you an aura bordering on white, and in addition, wisdom within your mind beyond your dreams. Your final initiation has ended this night.

Question to Michael: At the last meeting on February 3rd, I was told by Michael's message that something would happen, and it did not happen. I would like to know what went wrong, or what did I do wrong?

Answer: Within Our message to you last month you did not hear the second part of Our Words. Although We said that We shall transport you astrally aboard ship for healing, We also requested daily meditations for you to energize yourself to reinforce the healing you had received. This you have not done. You must understand. My Child, the intense desire for well-being must totally emanate from your vibrations, as well as the assistance We may give you. We cannot do it all alone. We must involve your own free will and your desires. Think in retrospect. Look into your mind and into your heart, for the answer is there. We say to you once again, when you return home this night We shall once again move your astral body aboard ship for healing. However, if you do not consistently make the effort yourself, the healing energies shall dissipate as before.

Question to Sananda: Yesterday at 12: 05 p.m., I was aware of an energy drain within me. Can you explain this?

Answer: You are one of the Ancients. As such, you are subject to periodic attacks, although you carry a high level of protection around you. It is Divine Law that you be open to these bursts of negativity, more as a testing situation of your power, your growth and your devotion to your Father. Be aware: protect yourself at all times.

Question to Michael: How long will the effects of the solar eclipse last, or have they abated already?

Answer: The effects of the solar eclipse shall last for another month or so. The intensity will be at a much lower level. I would say that, at this present time the effect of the eclipse has basically ebbed to the point where it should not interfere with your normal life. It will have a far more lasting effect on those steeped in negativity.

Question to Michael: Is this physical problem that I'm having now part of my total cleansing?

Answer: Partially yes, and partially no. The malformation of the vertebrae located at the fifth lumbar is a reminder of your mortality that you shall carry with you always, to keep you tied to the Earth plane, so to speak. The balance of it shall be with you as long as you allow these types of vibrations to affect your life and your stability. When you decide to shake them off the other problems shall disappear.

Question to Michael: What level of cleansing have I reached?

Answer: It is not the level of cleansing that you have reached. It is a level of development that has required an additional cleansing at this time.

You are faced with the question that you have not asked, so we shall answer it for you just the same. You have reached the black belt of energy, and soon the ray of Fuchsia shall rise over the black for you. When that occurs, the cleansing shall have been completed.

Question to Spirit: I am concerned as to the illness of my wife, the effect it will have, and how long it will be present. This I ask in relation to what I fee] is my work in the New Age Group.

Answer: We come to you in total peace and love. Many of you who walk our Father's Path are consistently faced with obstacles to overcome. Sometimes it seems to you in your minds that the more you prove your devotion to God, the harder the obstacles become. Perhaps this is true. However, we must understand that all situations that arise that seem to be a block or a wall prohibiting us from doing our work are merely things for us to overcome.

We cannot, in all sincerity, discuss your wife's illness. It is all part of what you must experience at this time. Let us just ask you to maintain your vibrations and their flow. Accept what is occurring at the moment it occurs. In the end you shall rise above it all. In the end all shall be as it must be.

Question to Michael: I have just returned from a long trip. I have been traveling for the past five years from place to place. I want to try to settle down somewhere, but my energies and vibrations seem to be going in all different directions. I need insight to find a niche or where I am supposed to be. Can you help me with this?

Answer: We suggest that you stop running from yourself for a moment. Sit and take some time alone. Look inside and see what it is you are made of, and what it is you are consistently running from, hoping to find, or trying to escape from. The answer to your question does not lie with Me. The answer lies with you. You must allow yourself to experience your feelings and your desires. Listen to your thoughts and to your impressions. Then you shall come to the point where your running shall cease. You shall have found your own direction. When this happens, then We shall be pleased to teach and assist you.

Question to Michael: A number of months ago I asked for some help on a dream or communication I had received relating to a ship that had landed. I was given directions to a mountain. You told me that I had to figure it out for myself, but not much has happened. A few weeks ago, I went into my classroom, and on the blackboard was a facsimile of the mountain I had seen. Are these connected or just a coincidence?

Answer: I wish I could say otherwise, but it was a coincidence. However, use the coincidence to your advantage. Perhaps it shall stimulate a renewed effort on your part to visualize the mountain in meditation to bring you the answer you seek.

Question to Murvin: Is it possibly true that the U.S. government has been using their space shuttle for experiments unknown to the people? It seems to me this could be true.

Answer: While it is true that your government is using your space shuttle for certain types of experiments, they are of a valid, scientific nature. They are not something that should concern anyone.

Question to Michael: Will the project I am working on be funded?

Answer: At this time the vibrations indicate that it will be funded. We do anticipate some type of problems arising that may seem to delay the funding for a while. At one point all may seem to be lost, but We do believe that it shall come to pass. Once the energies are committed for the funding, the project shall be successful.

Question to Sananda: The disaster that happened recently in Ghyana: there was a channeling that recently came from Texas, and I was asked by other Light Workers to supply some information if I could. There seemed to be a veil around the channeling. The rumor was that it was a different purpose for this incident than seemed to be on the surface. Does it have anything to do with the U.S. government and Russia?

Answer: It may seem strange to most of you, but the souls that perished within this incident were part of a karmic pattern, for they have done this before. It was a total karmic involvement having no relation to political or any other type of situation. This is the third time this event has occurred within this group of souls. We do say that some of those who perished did so, not consciously knowing they were to perish, having been tricked into death. The karma as told involved the group as a unit, not as individuals.

Same question continued: May I clarify the reason for the question? The veil I mentioned has to do with the karma. I could not accept the rumor from Texas. That is why I could not give them a clear answer.

Answer: The karmic situation was, in fact, the cause for the veil.

Question to Sananda: Is this a good time to start on a new project which includes fund raising and investigation, starting a whole series of programs?

Answer: There is never a wrong time to start God's Work. Every morning when you arise is the perfect day to spread your love. When you have spent your energies and planted your seeds in the proper soil, all shall flow.

Question to Michael: Will you speak on the current events concerning Iran and what is happening internally?

Answer: The situation in Iran shall become far more severe before it becomes better. It shall put the world to a test. The situation shall become highly inflammable in relation to many other nations. In the end, there shall be another revolution, and a new more liberal government shall be established in Iran.

Question to Michael: Recently I started a project in design, a new gas saver. What I am interested in knowing is will it be successful, and is it properly designed?

Answer: I am sorry to deny you the proper answer to your question. If we were to advise you relating to the proper structure of this machine, we would be interfering with the normal path of progress within your society. You may, if you wish, seek spiritual advice from within, for this is your right.

Question to Michael: The effectual activity of Light Workers in the East who use precipitation for food, fuel and transportation, will that be part of the activity of the school that will be started soon in Mexico, or does it have to be achieved individually?

Answer: It is something that must be achieved by every individual, especially in the early stages of the development of the school.

We must take this opportunity now to end our session for tonight. Each of us sends you our energies, our Blessings, and our love. We ask you to continue your growth.

Bless you in our Father's Name.

Chapter 8

Christos: Spiritual Initiations

Bless you. This is Christos.

It is indeed a night of joy and of celebration. We speak to you for the first time in total unity, having undergone complete assimilation of self. The name, Christos, signifies the total unity of the Christ vibration with the other aspects of the soul at the conscious level. There shall be others who will be spiritually called Christos.

Since our last meeting the vibrations have been in quite a turmoil. There has been much indecision, sickness and frustration manifesting itself without recourse or alternative action. This has partially been due to the position of the planets, and partially due to the fact that certain areas of growth may no longer be postponed, pushed aside, or held in abeyance. The time has come when what will be done must be done. It is along this vein of information that we wish to speak to you this evening.

We are going to discuss with you the process of spiritual initiations and how they affect the development of your lives relating to both the physical and spiritual planes.

The total cycle of growth, from the time one commits oneself to God's Path, consumes a full nine-year cycle. This involves a series of six levels of spiritual initiations or steps along the path to fulfillment. The journey is indeed a difficult one. It is important that you understand that all are not subjected to the same type of testing, system of pressure, or the same degree of learning.

The severity of the initiations depends primarily on the nature of the task or mission that the individual soul has been selected for upon the completion of their initiations. Every soul that completes the sixth initiation does so against the odds. For every soul that reaches completion, fifty-three do not. Before we begin to discuss the rewards and benefits for those that pass, we wish to discuss the effects and lives of those that do not pass, for they are of a far greater number.

Growth and knowledge are an eternal blessing that never fade. The vibrations become an integral part of every soul for the balance of time. Why then is a soul chosen to begin a series of initiations, to have spent energy on it if it is felt that it shall not endure? All those who have a desire to commit themselves to God are entitled to the opportunity to do so. There are those who endure who were not expected to endure. The strength of mind and free will and determination are the unknown factors that determine completion.

(You will please note that I did not use the word failure, for there is no failure.)

It is merely a choice of free will. No one has ever fallen by the side in failure. It has been their choice to release themselves from their commitment, often from feeling the lack of ability to stand any additional pressure, or their lack of determination to fulfill their spiritual destiny.

For example, if a soul has completed its fourth initiation, and in the midst of the fifth initiation decides that it can no longer endure or pursue its course, all knowledge and growth assimilated by the soul to that moment remain with the soul. It is Blessed and released from its commitment, allowed to continue its life and its path according to its free will.

It is important for you to understand never to fear, never to feel that some terrible misfortune shall overcome you if you are not capable of, or no longer have the desire to fulfill the program of spiritual learning that has been laid in front of you. During the course of our unification, we must, in all truth, relate to you that many times we have been but a hairs breath from throwing it all away. Blessedly, we are here, we are finished, and now we shall share our knowledge and our love with all mankind. Many have asked why the necessity for such severity of testing? I shall answer in a way that I have never answered before, for now is the time to relate the specific truth within this area.

Once a soul has reached a point within its development where it has achieved unification of all levels of consciousness, that union is with it for the balance of the incarnation and cannot be removed by Spirit or any other force. This means that if one is given this power and ability and at some time in the future decides to misuse it, to abuse it, or to leave his Father's Path, we are helpless to do anything to deter him from his wishes or abuses of this power and knowledge.

For this reason and this reason alone, all who strive to reach this fulfillment must prove to our Father beyond all doubt, a thousand times beyond all doubt, their total commitment to teach His Laws and His Love. Understand that Spirit has the knowledge of who shall be eternally committed. It is the individual soul that must have this awareness at the conscious level. This can only be achieved through experiencing exposure to all types and forms of situations that consistently test your devotion and strain it to attempt to pry you away from your Father. In this way a stronger and stronger bond is created.

The path one walks narrows considerably with each ensuing initiation. When one has reached the sixth level of initiation it is as if one is walking a thin trail up a lonely mountain spiraling ever upward. The trail becomes narrower and narrower until one is walking with one foot in front of the other at a snail's pace. One misstep and he shall certainly fall off the cliff. I have said this to you to symbolize the path of completion. As you grow in knowledge and learning your vibrations rise and increase in their sensitivity. They carry the properties of becoming increasingly sensitive to negativity and vulnerable to the negativity.

There are only three people within this circle who have not passed their fourth-level initiation. There are nine who shall enter their fifth-level initiation before the summer season. There are three who shall enter the sixth level, and four who have begun the sixth initiation within the last three months.

I wish you to understand that Spirit is totally aware of the trials and the severity of reaction of many of the tests you undergo. If you have reached a point within your pattern of growth that faces you to an insurmountable wall, avail yourself of the experience, the sympathy, the compassion of one of your brothers or sisters to share your problems with and seek their assistance. No one must walk along. All are here to help one another. If it was not anticipated that each and every one of you would not reach unification within your soul, you would not be present at these sessions. You would not be drawn to our vibrations. You are here because it is known that you shall complete, you shall fulfill.

Upon your fulfillment this is what awaits you: You shall have at your disposal the universal or cosmic knowledge, to have a thought or question relating to any subject, and within moments to have the answer implanted in your conscious mind for your use: to carry within your vibrations, manifested consciously within your aura, the energies of the Spirit, the energies of Love. These energies will draw to you all those who have a need for your love.

These are the tools that you need: the knowledge and the Divine Love. It is important for you all to understand that all abilities and spiritual gifts that are bestowed upon you have been earned by you.

Whatever you receive you are entitled to through work, through effort, through devotion. Accept your abilities totally. Never feel that you are undeserving of a spiritual gift. If it were so, in God's Truth, you would not receive.

These are the words I bring you in my message tonight. Before we proceed to the questions and answers there are the energies of someone, a friend, a counselor, an advisor to all of you eventually within your search for fulfillment. We bring you the energies of the soul who sits at the Hand of God whose responsibility is the planet Earth, who is known of you.

Solomon: The Battle of Growth

Bless you, My Children. This is Solomon.

It has been two years since I have spoken through the soul of my Father, my son. We have shared much together. There are those in this room who do battle with me now, a battle of growth, a battle of learning, a battle of strength of mind and will of steel. To me falls the responsibility given to me by our Father to prepare those Children of Light selected for total fulfillment and unification. I have taught and tested untold thousands of souls. All, without exception, have tried many times to destroy me or to remove me from their vibrations. Yet, in the end, all has been love. All is always accomplished with love as the end result. So, I say to you, when the time comes to each and every one of you when, in your meditations, you are requested to make a verbal commitment to our Divine Father. If you do so of your own free will, within a period of four weeks I shall be with you. I shall teach you the higher truths and begin your program of development and completion. This may be the last time I talk to you with such tenderness, for indeed I am a stern teacher, but always with love, and I Bless you.

Questions and Answers

Now it is time for the period of questioning. We ask Blossom to act as monitor. You may proceed at this time.

Question: Does the name "Caspus" have any particular meaning for me?

Answer: The name relates to a past incarnation in the year 17,546 B.C. The vibrations of this soul are partially involved within your soul, and partially within another soul. It will cause an effect on your spiritual growth within the next six or seven weeks. This will be the force that will begin to solidify many scattered energies that have been confusing you for the past several months.

Question: How am I doing on my mission that I was given a few months ago?

Answer: Are you satisfied with your progress on your mission?

("No")

Then we say to you that you are doing quite poorly.

Question: I have been given some information from the group in Tucson. An announcement was made that on Easter Sunday evening a group will make an ascent aboard the Dove. I have been requested to join them and wish to know if I should make this trip.

Answer: We take the liberty of answering your question with a question. Based upon your experiences within the past six months, would you feel comfortable departing for this mission without receiving your own personal confirmation?

("No")

It is a beautiful thing to receive invitations. It is a more positive thing to receive confirmations.

Question: I would like to know who "Ara-Michael" is. He visited me about four or five years ago in a spirit embodiment. I would like to know who that person is in relation to myself.

Answer: You have received a projection of energies from the Father of this Universe. A facet of this is named Michael who brought to you the Light, the love and the vibrations to make you aware that you are a Child of Light: to begin to open the door to your spiritual growth and prepare you for higher vibrations: to stir inside you the recognition of the energies of God within you.

Question: Can you tell me what connection my teacher, Hiram Abif, has with my soul growth at this time?

Answer: Within a period of four to five months your teacher shall no longer be with you. You shall have reached a level of vibrations that shall bring to you the services of a higher elevated Master. You shall be receiving your new Master, Athena. She will help you project vibrations of universal love to all those who walk within your aura. She shall teach you many truths and wisdom.

Question: Any comment you would care to make of a specific nature about me at this time?

Answer: Yes. You are still playing a game with your life. You know what you are capable of doing, and yet you do not do it. You know the spiritual potential in your mind, and you use it when you choose and deny it when you wish to. This shall continue for you as long as you allow it and refuse to accept the responsibility for yourself. I realize that commitment is sometimes a most difficult decision to make. It requires a firm step forward, and often necessitates leaving behind the crutches that offer so much support. It is a necessary thing to do if you are to look at yourself and find peace. We would advise you to slow down long enough to see where you are. You may find that you can love yourself.

Question: I was asked by a spirit named "Miqui" to ask you to tell us about music with spheres. Can you tell us what that is about?

Answer: The music of the spheres relates to the vibrations of the worlds that send the music of God's Love to all souls as a form of enlightenment and healing.

Question: I feel that I have been receiving information from another planet in our solar system. May I have the name of the planet and the reason for this communication?

Answer: You have been receiving vibrations from the planet Jupiter. They have been coming to you because a portion of your energies and knowledge banks relate to and have experienced incarnations within these vibrations. It will be an experience of relearning knowledge from your past incarnations.

Question: For a long time, Jupiter and Saturn have been crossing my mind. They are very strong. The vibrations I receive make me nervous. Am I blocking a message from coming through?

Answer: My dear child, you are shaky and nervous because you do not allow yourself trust. Once again, we ask you to accept yourself totally and know that what comes to you is your truth. You have the ability to handle the information and knowledge that is trying to come to you. You are worthy of what you receive, or you would not receive it.

Question: Should I continue my pursuit of the past relating to WW1, writing and involving myself in this period?

Answer: By all means continue with this effort. Somewhere along the way there are messages to be heard and lessons to be learned as yet uncovered from that conflict. Many times, the energies of the past prove to be an important tool for the future. It is no accident that you are involved in this area. It is for a purpose. Know it and accept it, and you shall uncover much unknown information.

Question: A few days ago, I heard a voice call my name from behind me. I listened but did not hear anything else. Was this important to me?

Answer: It is of prime importance to you. It is the first sign of recognition from one of your teachers, a greeting to tell you that you are not alone at the conscious level, and soon the time shall come when your teacher will make his presence known to you. His name, by the way, is Jeramiah.

Question: I was here last August on my way to Sedona to do a clearing operation. My affirmation is that it is almost done at this time. Will you clarify this for me?

Answer: You are correct, and we Bless you for your work.

Question: A number of years ago I started on interplanetary communication. All of a sudden, I had a heart attack and almost passed. Was I going too far, too fast?

Answer: The end result was that you were going too fast. In truth, you were moving at a proper pace. It was only your lack of acceptance that created "too far, too fast".

Question: In meditation a few days ago, I saw myself being at an airport with some people around. I had the impression it had to do with space people. The number 800 came into my mind. What does it mean?

Answer: The vibrations of thoughts that came into your mind were what we call "slippage" from another level of vibrations. It came into your wavelength quite by accident. This does happen occasionally. It is like unconscious eavesdropping into another level of vibration.

Question: There is a brother who I work with. There have been a number of incidences in the last few months that seem to point to some interaction between us. I feel that I should confront him with this verbally. I don't know whether I have something to give him, learn from him, or is he being used without his knowledge. Can you comment on this please?

Answer: The involvement within the interchange of vibrations is related to his lessons, and his alone. We suggest you send him love. Use reflective energy to return all negativity: transmute it to love, and then he shall begin to grow.

Question: I deal with a man in a work situation that I have sent love to constantly for more than a year with not too much success. Am I doing it properly?

Answer: You are doing just fine. The only problem is his lack of recognition or unwillingness to accept. In order to survive within your work situation, learn to tolerate his vibrations. Allow him to be as he wishes but keep his vibrations from entering your aura.

Question: Last month Michael talked about sending love to the world. I wonder if you could elaborate on that. Is there anything specific we should do?

Answer: When one has begun to sit in meditation and has installed their protection around them, a few words projecting love and light to all of God's children shall serve effectively.

Question: I am having a difficult time making decisions in my life. Am I acting in the proper manner?

Answer: If your decisions were easy for you, they would truly be the wrong decisions. You are about to embark on a drastic change in the course of your life. Have faith within your mind and in your intuition. Do not allow your emotions to interfere with your sense of reason, and you shall reach the proper conclusions.

Question: Why did you say to me that I have just realized that I have come into full scope? I did that a while back. Are you saying that my understanding has been completed?

Answer: You are sitting here as a child with a new toy. At the same instant you acquired the toy you acquired an extremely heavy responsibility that goes along with it. We wish you to use it in the proper perspective and manner in which it was given to you. There is no joy, there is no elation, and there are no fireworks. All God's Gifts are accepted without change of a single vibration. As we have said before, you only receive what you have earned. Energy spent is returned without fanfare, and without fireworks.

Question: I feel that there is a message for me tonight. Is there?

Answer: There has been a message waiting for you for several months. Perhaps now you are ready to hear the words we wish to speak. You have walked into our vibrations on infrequent occasions over a period of many months. Yet you have known that you belong in these vibrations far more often. You have found reasons to avoid your responsibilities for your growth. You know who you are, as do we. We sit in great patience, and we shall stay here until the day comes when you, yourself, decide to accept your destiny. We say this to you with much love and anticipation.

We take this opportunity to bring our session for this night to a close. We ask that each and every one of you continue your search for another Child of Light to enhance this circle so that one day there shall be enough love to make this city a total spiritual center of the world.

We Bless you for your love.

Chapter 9

Christos and the 36 Rays

Bless you. This is Christos.

Once again, we welcome you to share in the vibrations of this Circle of Light. Without each and every one of you it truly does not exist.

Tonight is a very special evening. Later on, there shall be many questions asked that shall bring answers to all and shall reveal new areas of work to some and new goals to reach for others. We have this day the pleasure of bringing you the colors and the rays above the level of the twenty- second ray. We commence with the 23rd ray and end, for the time being, with the 36th ray.

The rays shall not be generally available to all of God's Children until the change of the planetary vibrations has been accomplished beginning in the year 1984. We relate them to you so you may become acquainted with them, perhaps attempt to invoke them. There are some of you who are capable of using these rays now. All of the rays are pearlized in color and banded in White Light for purity.

#23: A ray of five stripes: Three of red and two of silver, alternating.

#24: Lime Green: Basically, used for healing. One of the mainstays used for healings done aboard ship.

#25: Lemon Yellow: A ray of direct communication with Solomon.

#26: Silver Grey: Used for communication with those souls that comprise the White Brotherhood.

#27: Silvery Pink: Used for communication with the energies of Athena.

#28: A ray of five stripes: Three of powder blue and two of gold. This ray is used for interplanetary communication.

#29: Violet with gold flecks: A ray of communication with one known as Talmus. A ray of healing for perpetual health.

#30: Palest Orange: A ray for communication with God's Angels.

#31: Pale Blue flecked with silver stars: A ray of materialization.

#32: Palest of Green: A ray available to those who have been granted the use of Prana energy to heal with.

#33: Palest of Rose: Used to communicate with the Essence that has created the nature spirits.

#34: Palest of Violet: Used to communicate with the energies of Sananda.

#35: Whitest of White: The ray of communication with the Christ Spirit.

#36: This ray manifests itself as a thunderbolt, as a brilliant flash of all thirty-five colors consuming your entire being within its vibrations. With it comes the Love and Breath of our Divine Father.

We wish to speak to you for a moment relating to the seasons and the time of the year that is upon us. Mankind is prone to a regimented existence, to a seasonal form of life. We ask you to please remember not to hang a sign on your door, "I will return to God after summer vacation."

The next few months are going to prove to be extremely unsettled for many of you. You shall notice more and more every day those classmates, study mates, associates will be leaving their path, falling by the wayside. Show your concern but understand that it is their choice. Many shall not be able to find it in their hearts to have a strong enough devotion and dedication to pursue their spiritual path. Indeed, lessons shall become more intense. Try to accept your lessons lightly and in love. It is truly not necessary for you to experience pain and anguish. That is only preconditioning and programming. Be firm in your beliefs and your convictions, and your progress shall flow smoothly for you. Be aware that when you have reached a point, a stumbling block that is manifesting negativity to you, the chances are that it is of your own creation and your own refusal to accept something that has been projected to you in the proper manner.

The negative forces are becoming stronger and stronger. They fear more and more as the Light shines brighter and brighter. It shall continue to grow and shine until all the negativity has been subdued. Be aware of its presence, but

know that you can and shall overcome it.

Questions and Answers

Now it is time for the questions. We ask Blossom to act as monitor.

Question: Please explain "Talmus" to us.

Answer: Talmus is an extension of the energies of Peter, a very old ancient soul, who serves our Father in the capacity of performing the highest levels of healing and cleansing on this planet. His services are utilized in areas when one so incarnated has ahead of them a plan of work and destiny that requires them to be in total perfect health for the balance of their incarnation. To him falls the responsibility of maintaining this balance, both physically and spiritually.

Question: Could you please give me some insight into this skin condition I have acquired? Is it a rash? Should I seek medical attention?

Answer: We feel that the skin condition is an allergic reaction that has taken hold of you at this time. We recommend packs of warm, raw milk over the area every three to four hours for a period of five days.

Question: In meditation the name "Naiel" came very clearly for me to bring to you. It appears that this name is a very significant soul that should be brought into your aura for you to work with. In the metaphysical dictionary it is referred to as "The house of the most high". Perhaps you might have something to say on this.

Answer: We most certainly do, and we Bless you most sincerely for initiating this vibration. We have experienced these vibrations this very day, and it shall please us to share the name "Naiel" and its significance to

all.

The name "Naiel" stands for the energies within the house of the Divine Father, for as each of us, as souls, carries with us our own sphere of vibrations, those who serve as our acquaintances and friends enter our sphere of vibrations to feel and touch and share and love. So, it is with our Father. It is a most difficult and dangerous journey. The road to the house of Naiel is zealously guarded, and the entranceway is a very fine, thin stream of vibrations. May I say at this time that it is our fervent prayer that each of you within this circle shall one day enter this portal.

Question: Do you have a message for me?

Answer: It is indeed a great pleasure to feel your vibrations within this circle. Your life shall now truly begin to follow its appointed path. Already many new levels of awareness and energy have begun to filter down to you. You have indeed made your total commitment to God. You have severed your unnecessary connections with the material world and have shown the confidence and the faith within your love for your Father to commit yourself totally to His Path. Because of this the rewards have already begun to flow and shall continue to do so as long as you walk in God's Light.

We ask you, during your meditations, to allow the higher rays to flow through your being. This will help in your expansion and open new horizons for your healing energies and your work. New areas of material for you to teach shall begin to come to you.

Question: Which of the new the permission to use?

Answer: The first 22 rays are at your disposal at this time. Within the newer range of rays we have presented this evening, you have the capacity to use #25, #28 and #31.

Question: I was told that you have a message for me. Also, I would like to know when my communication relating to my projects will resume.

Answer: The communication on your projects shall not resume until the vibrations within your residence have been restored to love and peace. You are operating in a vibration that cannot tolerate the type and amount of negativity present in your home structure. You must realize that sensitivity will not enter a negative vibration. We suggest that you expedite harmony at home as soon as possible.

Now for the second part of your question. We do indeed have a message for you. We wish to say that your Light shines more every day. Your devotion and your love for your fellow man is becoming stronger as each day passes. In a few weeks a new avenue of study and research shall be planted in your mind. You shall no longer be involved with basic instruction. Leave that to others.

Question: Can you tell me something of a specific nature and purpose for the work that and I are to do together?

Answer: You have had your vibrations torn to shreds and been thoroughly cleansed in the past three or four weeks. We send you love to ease the pain and the bewilderment that surely must have come over you. There was no other choice, for the time was not available.

Now your vibrations are more relaxed and clear, and you shall become what you believe you are.

For the moment, the work involving the two of you is as follows: It is to build a unity to present to others as an example, and to build a vibration so others may come to hear and share. From that point there shall open for you several avenues of pursuit. We do not wish to describe them for you. You must experience them for yourself.

Question: I have a condition that has recurred in my body that I have no control of. Is it brought on by my higher self, or has someone imposed it on me without my knowledge?

Answer: It is a condition that you have not totally released from the last time. Search your mind for the experiences that you have endured prior to the recurrence of this illness. Find out what prompted you to allow this to reappear. Do not feel that someone is imposing this upon you, thus relieving yourself from being responsible for the illness. It is not so. Be truthful: release the illness and your good health shall return.

Question: I had a series of questions I wished to ask you before the session started. But since then, something else has come to me that I wish to confirm. There was a declaration made by me in October of last year having to do with banding the auras of the Children of Light. I feel that I am supposed to reaffirm this before the full moon this month. Can you confirm this please?

Answer: You place an extremely heavy responsibility upon your shoulders at all times. For your unfailing willingness to do so, you are truly Blessed. We say that it would be proper for you to take the action as you have been inspired to do.

Question: I have two questions, one relating to a friend who questions me relating to reincarnation with statements that we have only eight or ten lives and asks for proof that reincarnation exists. I am at a loss as how to answer him. Secondly, I am concerned as to how I should handle the sickness with my wife.

Answer: In relation to your first question, do not put yourself in a position where one may make demands upon you to prove things to them. If you have spoken your truth, and they cannot accept it, bless them and release them. There are many others willing to hear your truth and accept it. We are not here to have our truth tested in judgment. We are here to live and share it with those who desire to hear it.

In relation to your wife, send her all the love, as we have done and shall continue to do. Give her strength and know that you are doing all you can to help her. The rest, ask your Father to do.

Question: Could Naiel have some connection to the 36th ray, or is it basically kundalini energy?

Answer: He is directly aligned and connected with the 36th ray.

Question: Am I properly following my path at this time?

Answer: It is our pleasure to say that you are where you should be at this time. We realize that at times you are impatient with the lack of conscious growth, but you must understand that we do not wish to overwhelm you. We wish to teach and to help you grow. You shall receive what you are capable of handling. You have much knowledge and learning within the banks of your soul.

Question: Could you shed some light on what I am going through at home at this time, and how much longer it must go on?

Answer: It will go on as long as you allow it to go on. When you reach the point in your life when you understand your worth and the love that many others have for you, then you will refuse to allow this situation to endure. Until that time all that befalls you, you are allowing and accepting. As long as you remain in this situation it shall continue. Have the strength to know that God shall provide for you and fulfill your life.

Question: How can I best help our brother?

Answer: You can help him by understanding that he is in the throes of his own lessons. Send him wisdom, love, and allow him to learn his own lessons. That is how it must be. Do not try to mother him, for in truth, he must work this through by himself. It is he that has, against our advice and the advice of others, placed himself in the position he is in today. We do not wish to seem heartless or stern, but within his position as a Child of Light he has accepted a level of responsibility and must accept what comes along with it or be left by the side.

Question: I have a question relating to these entities I see at night for several months. I become afraid and send them away before I find out who they are and what they want. Do you have any suggestions for me so I can find a way to communicate with them?

Answer: Basically, many of the entities that come to you and seem to frighten you are manifestations of your own fears. Concentrate more on releasing your fears relating to yourself. Try to establish the strength within your own personality. Then you shall fear nothing. You shall know that all who come to you do so in God's Light.

Question: I have two questions. What ship was it that we saw this weekend, and on the trip, we are making, will we likely see more ships?

Answer: The ship you sighted was Jupiter #43. You shall see many others, for you have accepted their presence in your truth. It will be good for you both to go to this area, to climb the mountains and bring yourselves closer to pure vibrations, to feel the peace and the serenity.

Question: Why is it that Jeremiah has not made his presence known to me at the conscious level?

Answer: When you will release your vibrations to him in meditation and allow him to know that you desire this communication with him for growth and truth, when he is sure that it is not for ego, for enjoyment, then he shall come to you consciously. The connection is not from your choice, but from his. It shall come soon.

Question: Do you have any message for me?

Answer: We always have something to say to you. You have initiated the healing of your physical being. It shall not take place overnight. With the assistance of all those who love you and send you their energies along with your own determination and faith, all shall come to a positive conclusion. Continue your life as you are, growing and having faith. The pain shall become more severe and then shall ease and fade away.

Question: I came down with a condition that has been irritating my shoulders. I have tried everything. Why is it there, and how can I end this discomfort?

Answer: We are feeling the irritations of a mild arthritis in that area. We suggest that you send pink or rose light to that area in meditation for cooling and healing.

Question: In one of my meditations concerning the elusive mountain I have been looking for, the top crest of the mountain was shown to me. On either side of the crest was a golden river flowing down. What does this signify?

Answer: The symbology behind the golden rivers relates to what awaits you when you reach the crest of your mountain of growth and learning. The wealth of all shall flow at your feet. Keep climbing up and looking for your mountain but know that it is in front of your nose.

Question: A friend of mine has been working on the correlation of sound and color and has put together charts on the first thirteen rays. I wondered if they are accurate?

Answer: There are slight miscalculations on the 11th and 13th rays. The others are accurate.

Question: Have you anything to say to me?

Answer: We feel that it is important for you to begin serious concentrated effort to achieve spiritual communication. You are ready for more highly developed levels of learning and truth to come to you through Spirit. You are spiritually lazy. Please correct this.

Question: Is it likely that my parents will be changing some of their major attitudes as they are exposed to our growth? Is this a long-term process? Will it be done in their lifetime?

Answer: Your growth will effect a change in their thinking. Whether it will be completed or not depends on their acceptance. In any case, accept it as it is, and allow it to flow without any interference on your part. When they ask a question, answer it. Encourage, don't push.

Question: When you mentioned the healing through the Prana, I blacked out. Have I been working with this vibration in my healing?

Answer: Yes.

Question: Will I soon be able to work in the field of the New Age?

Answer: When you will totally release the guilt that you surround yourself with. Until that time, you must amass your energies in sufficient strength to allow you to achieve this growth.

Question: Early today I was speaking a foreign language in meditation. It seemed to be Russian. What meaning does it have?

Answer: You have a Master who comes to you presenting himself from an incarnation in that country and period. This denotes an important incarnation for him. It will bear a strong relation to the type of teaching and information he will present to you. His name is Radjinski. You have the ability for a high degree of development. Be very careful. Be on your guard against an ego involvement, for the tendency is there in your growth pattern.

Question: Several weeks ago, in meditation I encountered one who called himself Lanto. That name was followed by a name, Lantu. I said that I would ask you for confirmation, and he laughed at me. Could you elaborate please?

Answer: The proper spelling is Lantu. He laughed at you for it seemed ridiculous to him that you should need to confirm anything relating to his presence. He is very old and ancient. You will find him tough, stern and yet soft and warm. He will teach you many things.

Question: Can you give me some idea about the business I am trying to start?

Answer: I wish I could tell you that your path will be initially easy and fruitful, but there will be much work and struggle involved. The timing does not matter. A beginning must be made. If you endure in faith, it shall succeed.

Question: I have not been able to communicate with one of my Master teachers for some time. His name is Alonzopan. What does this mean?

Answer: Alonzopan is no longer within your vibrations. There is a Master by the name of Dorina who shall be with you in several weeks.

Question: During light meditation the other day I sang a song. Could you comment on where it came from?

Answer: We would prefer, as with so many lessons, that you procure this information from your teachers. Do your own research. You shall find the answer, and it will have more meaning to you.

We must take this opportunity to close our session for this night. We offer all of you our love and our Blessings. We ask you to be ever alert, ever constant, ever flowing on your path of growth and love. Bless you.

Chapter 10

Christos: Eternal Life

We Bless you my brothers and sisters. This is Christos.

As most of you are aware, the pace of vibrations circulating through your atmosphere is increasing daily. It shall continue to do so with increasing rapidity. It is basically toward this purpose and topic that we wish to speak to you tonight.

We have discussed with you the elevation of the basic vibrations on the planet Earth beginning in the year 1984. We are sure in the minds of all exists the question, "what will become of those who have, by that time, not accepted their spirituality, not become aware of the Light within them?" So, we will tonight try to explain to you the course of events as they shall occur in relation to those children who have not come to realization or to an awareness of their spirituality.

Many, many billions of years ago when the plans for the creation of this Universe were initiated and developed, the year of 1984 which draws upon us was chosen as a year, a critical year for the raising of the vibrations upon the surface of this planet: and so, within the evolution of this Universe the energies towards total existence were manifested and duly recorded. Nothing shall occur that shall alter the manifestation of these energies, for it is part of the evolution of this planet and this Universe. Those who sit in meditation and try to alter the energy patterns of this planet are indeed drawing karma upon themselves for interfering where they have no right to interfere. This decision is not theirs.

Life and existence is eternal. If an incarnated soul does not choose to grow and become aware of its identity, then it shall indeed be left back to take the class over again. In any event the lessons and growth will be achieved and learned, for this is progress and evolution. The violence that may begin to erupt within nations, within cities and communities within the next several years will not be recognized by most as a war of vibrations, or a war of compatibility with the energies that people breathe and partake to keep their life support system working. There will be just unrest, agitation, anger and depressions. I do not wish to frighten you, to intimidate you, nor to intimate that there shall be wholesale war and slaying, for it shall not be so.

It has been in preparation for this time that those of you who have become aware of your purpose are here. For those who have dedicated themselves to their spiritual path have been prepared by undergoing a series of initiations, lessons or tests that have, at times, seemed most severe to you, but it is what you must face and endure.

It is the rebellion, and the obstacles, and the jeers, and the denials and the fears of mankind that you shall have to overcome. Always know that your greatest tool is total love. There are many of you who have within the past several months, begun to be aware of the love vibration that emits from your being. We have heard you share and relate your experiences in class and otherwise, about the people that approach you and begin to confide in you, to question you. This is your mission.

I do not pretend to sit here and say that every soul incarnated at this time shall be saved, shall grow, shall acclimate themselves to the new vibration, for this is a superhuman, impossible task to achieve. All I ask is that you do your best, and that you know in your hearts and in your minds that you, as an individual, shall rise above. You know that your Father is with you. He shall protect and care for you.

There are no spiritual accidents, not even one, for if there were, it would cause an incredible imbalance of the cosmic energies. Whatever occurs, occurs exactly at its appointed time and place, to whatever degree it has been planned, with the desired result as anticipated.

Over the past seven or eight years many Children of Light have entered our vibrations to study, to learn and to share. Many of them are no longer within our circle of Light, for they have fallen by the wayside. For all that leave their path there are always several alternates, for the required number of aware Children of Light shall always be constant.

This planet shall not be destroyed and shall not pass out of existence within this century. It is the spiritual vibrations of this planet that shall undergo a change. If, however, by the year 2,222 A.D. this planet is not walking a total spiritual path with unity between all mankind, at that time the Children of Light shall be physically removed from the surface of this planet to an area of higher, purer vibrations to continue their growth.

There are many among you who shall walk during your current incarnation for many years beyond the normal span of life. This will enable you to complete your mission and your work. There are several of you within the circle in whom the physical aging process has already begun to be stabilized.

All I have said to you I do not wish you to discuss with those who will cast negativity upon your truth. I wish you to file it away in your minds and not dwell on it. Continue your lives as you are leading them. These are the words I bring you this night.

Before we begin the question-and-answer period, we have a special visitor who wishes to speak a few words of love and sharing with you.

Talmus

These are the energies of Talmus, and I Bless you.

Le us all close our eyes for a few moments so each of you can feel and sense my presence.

This is the first time that I have spoken thusly in many, many centuries. I am here at the request of our Divine Father to enlighten you in the area of my function for you, and for the balance of the Children of Light. I am as a fine powder that polishes the stone and gives it its radiance and its brilliance. To me falls the task of removing the imperfections to allow a soul to become totally united with self.

Perhaps of all Spirit, I am the most honored and the most rewarded. When my work is done, if I could, I would have tears of joy and pleasure in my eyes, for a completed soul is the most beautiful sight to behold. Each of you shall someday come to know me, to feel my vibrations blending with yours. Then you shall know that you have reached the point within your growth that you are approaching fulfillment. It shall be the time for you to give thanks and to Bless your Father for His Grace.

All of you are here within this sanctuary, within this sphere of energy, for it is here at this vibration, that you are to grow, to nurture and to mature. There are five within this room whom I have the honor of serving at this time. There are three who shall feel my energies before this month passes. It would please me greatly to have all of you standing in line waiting for my services. Use me as one of your goals, as a point for you to strive for, as an incentive for you to develop your minds so that you may fulfill your destinies.

I take your leave and I Bless you in our Divine Father's Name.

Question and Answers

Now it is time for the questioning. We ask Stuart to act as monitor.

Question: Do you have a special message for me tonight?

Answer: You are resting on a plateau in your development at this time. Much knowledge and growth is being assimilated by you at the subconscious level. You can expect to resume conscious growth and experiences within the next three to four weeks. This will occur at a much-increased pace and level. Enjoy the respite while you can.

Question: Is it correct that the affirmation that was brought to my knowledge that a certain portion of my own spiritual hierarchy has been causing some disruption, some mayhem?

Answer: The disruption within your energies and within your spiritual path at this time are indeed being initiated by your Masters. However, the cause of the disruption is yours. It rests on you to look back to see where you have strayed, where you have allowed an episode of guilt to descend upon you for something that you are not responsible for. You must realize that at this point in your development your path has become very narrow. The leeway for mistakes, the leeway for negativity is growing smaller and smaller. The situation is yours to alleviate.

Question: Recently I had a dream whereby I was given three green tickets. I wonder if you could shed some light on what those tickets mean. Are they all mine, or do they belong to my children as well?

Answer: The three green tickets symbolize to you a release of the three corners of thyself: the mind, body and soul, to allow you now to pursue your spiritual growth. You have recently undergone a release in your life to cleanse you of negativity and to release you from vibrations that have held you down for so many years. This dream was of the nature of a confirmation for you, to assure you that now you are free to pursue you path to fulfillment.

Question: My brother and I have been wondering where we have been in the past and why we are together now. Also, what are we going to do together in the future? Can you shed some light on this?

Answer: You have experienced five incarnations in the past with your brother. This is the second relationship where you are brother and sister. The other three times you have been sisters. You are here together in this life for the following reason: The lesson is your brother's, not yours. Out of the relationship and out of the strength and direction that you shall provide for him, he must come to a point in his life where he severs this relationship but severs it with love and pursues his path totally by himself. We do not wish to infer that it is improper for you to assist him at this time. However, when the time comes for the release, he must make it. This is the lesson in the relationship.

Question: The last few days I have spent a great deal of time with another man. It seems as though I was finding myself being extremely angry all of the time. Do I deserve a reprimand for this, or is it something in him that I was reacting to?

Answer: You are within the beginning of a change of level of vibrations. It is reminiscent of the time you underwent the change of spiritual guidance and experienced a lost feeling. This change of vibrations will extend to your physical and emotional structure as well. It is suggested that you just bear with it, knowing that soon it shall pass, and your growth shall continue.

Question: I am told that there is some information that you can give me about the path I am to pursue this summer.

Answer: You are to begin to take students to you and teach. You are at the point in your growth when you must start more firmly believing who you are, and then become that person. Procrastination must come to an end. You must make this commitment to yourself and to God, for there is a great destiny that awaits you. We feel that you are aware of this, but that you truly do not want to hear it, as you do not know if you can handle it. The only way you shall find out is to try but know that you shall have much assistance and love along your path. All that is necessary is for you to make the first step. We are here, as are many others in this room, should you need a friend for advice or love.

Question: A week ago, last Friday before I went to sleep, I had a visitation. At first it was welcome, but then seemed to turn into a struggle. I was hoping you could shed some light on this.

Answer: The struggle is indeed within yourself, between you and you. You are in a stage of questioning, of testing and validating as you should be. Do not feel that all visitation, meditation and communication must be warm and loving. It is all designed for growth and understanding. You must sort out your truth from that which you cannot accept, then begin to have the faith within yourself in that which you have adopted as your truth.

Question: As I am going through a very mixed-up period for some time now, could you tell me how I am doing, and is my course correct?

Answer: You have taken a giant step forward within your growth. Your desire to move to the vibrations which are present in the Phoenix area to find your answers has been a positive step. If you will remember to walk slowly and assimilate slowly, all shall be well. You must overcome this tendency you have to want to take it in at one moment. Learn and grow in peace and assimilate the knowledge every step along the way.

Question: I know of two past incarnations when Talmus and I were on the High Council together. Were there more than those two in your awareness, or was that it?

Answer: There has been a third one dating back to the time of Mu. There was also one within the confines of Atlantis.

("What about the Mars experience with Talmus?")

We believe this to have been a spiritual relationship not involving physical incarnation. There will be another association when this present incarnation has been completed, a lasting celebration.

("On the High Council again or as spiritual guides?")

It shall be in the capacity of a farewell party, for the energies of your soul are about to leave this Universe to transcend to a new area of evolvement and growth. He shall serve to prepare you for this journey.

Question: I feel that I have a fear of dying before I complete my spiritual growth and think that this is limiting my growth. Is this true, and if it is, what can I do about it?

Answer: When you rise every morning and get out of bed to pursue the course of events during the day, know in your heart that it may be your last day on Earth, as it may be for all. Use that day to the best advantage and grow as much as possible during that day. God can ask no more of you. Do not concern yourself with setting limits upon your growth, with completing your growth pattern within this incarnation. You do have several more incarnations after this one before you reach fulfillment. Concern yourself with the now, grow from there.

Question: I recently learned that soon I will be able to pursue my spiritual life every day. It is something I have been working on since I first set foot on this path. It is not clear to me exactly how I am going to do this and earn a living. Can you shed some light?

Answer: The transition from the normal working pattern to the total spiritual involvement for you shall not occur suddenly, but slowly and gradually. It is preferable that it happen this way so as not to put undue financial pressure or strain upon you. If you will allow all to flow in the direction that you are flowing now, you shall not even realize that the transition is being made.

Question: Do you have any suggestions for me regarding meditation?

Answer: We suggest that you begin a program of meditating within the vibrations of the higher rays. It will enhance your communication and begin to elevate your basic vibrations. Meditate with the colors of the rays from #23 to #36, using one or two at a session. This will familiarize you with their vibrations and enable you to eventually assimilate them.

Question: Do you have any information about how (Name) is doing on his mission so far?

Answer: He will return to Phoenix within the next several months a much wiser and perhaps more realistic individual. He has to this date, experienced much grief, pleasure and enlightenment. We feel that he has used part of this time for self-analysis within the area of his own interpretations of the word of Spirit. If he achieves no other growth, no other purpose than this, then the sojourn was well worth the time and the effort. We Bless you for your concern.

Question: Could you please tell me how I have been doing on my mission?

Answer: It would be most desirable for you, as it would be for many of you within the circle, to find time to consciously apply your knowledge and vibrations to help others. You are at the level of growth where it is necessary to begin to share. Your hands possess great healing abilities, but they must be used for it to continue to grow and develop.

Question: You mentioned earlier that a guest would say a few words. I have a feeling of very heavy energy, more so than I have ever felt before within me coming from this circle. Is there a correlation?

Answer: You have come here from another state to sit here this night. Part of the purpose that you are here is to experience the energies from this circle, then to return to share with your own circle and enhance their growth and knowledge, and so on. This is how all circles shall grow and grow.

Question: I have a question concerning the Rainbow Gathering, on its function and what I might achieve there this year.

Answer: You shall meet a man at the festival this year. I believe his name is (Name). He shall become a dear friend with whom you shall become spiritually involved. As for the rest of it, we ask you to please proceed with caution and protect yourself at all times for there will be negativity present at the festival. The energies of jealousy and resentment are strong within that area at this time. We do encourage you to attend, for there will be many beautiful children present at the festival.

Question: Recently I have been introduced to and begun an involvement working with precious gems. I was wondering if you could comment on what part they play in my growth?

Answer: We would prefer that you acquire a book relating to gems and their vibrations. Acquire your own answers within this area, for this too is part of your growth.

Question: I came in my reading upon the statement that the Law of Karma, the Law of Cause and Effect, does not exist. Is this true? Why, if it is true, have I believed otherwise?

Answer: What you call the Law of Karina is a by-product of the Law of Cause and Effect, for if we do not have a reaction from any action, we would not have a lesson to grow from and a vibration to achieve. The terminology is quite unimportant. It is the understanding and the growth that adds to the vibrations of the soul.

Question: If I am not to hope to achieve spiritual salvation in this incarnation, what is my purpose of this incarnation?

Answer: Your prime reason for coming into this incarnation is to learn and accept yourself in love, and to appreciate your value to yourself and to others. To help you achieve this result you have been and shall continue to be exposed to many situations that shall, at times, seem to be designed to hold you back. All of this is designed to build strength within you. When this has been achieved, you shall truly begin to grow spiritually and live within the spiritual vibration. Understand that growth and fulfillment is a lengthy, slow process. There are many levels of initiation to fulfill. I t is quite rare that one has the capacity, the fortitude and the strength to endure all of them in a short span of incarnations.

And now we bring the session for tonight to a close.

We Bless you for sharing your energies with us this night in our Father's Name.

Chapter 11

Bless you. This is Christos.

Before I begin there is someone whose vibrations are also a part of my soul, who will manifest himself and say a few words to you relating to the topic for tonight's discussion. These are energies that you have not experienced before, so be aware and enjoy them.

Moses on Incarnation

My name is known to you as Moses, and I Bless you.

I have been given this opportunity to say a few words to you this evening in relation to tonight's lecture, for who but I, has experienced more totally and fully the story of the evolution of man on Earth.

The evolutionary process has almost reached the fifth level of vibrations, for evolution in truth, bears no relation to physical appearance to more beautifully shaped figures or handsomely shaped men. Evolution relates to a growth and increase of vibrations.

I am not in the habit of making predictions, but I say to you that within the next three to four years mankind in total, shall indeed begin to understand and to learn the truth of Creation. He shall learn man's role and his destinies on this planet, as well as many others throughout this Universe.

During the incarnation when I was called Moses, much of this truth was known to all, for all walked with our Father. The self-judgment that mankind had placed upon itself lost this knowledge at the conscious level for many thousands of years. Now, joyously, we are approaching the Light once again. I implore you all to lead your lives along God's Path, to continue your studies, to increase your awareness and help those who seek your help. Only in that way shall all mankind at last discover His Truth. I Bless you for allowing me a few moments to share with you this night.

Christos: Assimilation of Vibration

This is Christos.

The evolution of mankind has been in progress for many many billions of years. The word mankind does not refer to a physical male walking your planet. It refers to all souls experiencing incarnation with or without physical form. Our Divine Father's Laws are simple and yet in their simplicity they are so clearly defined that all is exact or will be as it is planned to be. The soul upon it's creation, must assimilate to its vibrations, all aspects of Divine Love. This is the entire purpose of the soul. Divine Love, a simple enough phrase, and yet the most complex phrase within the Universe, for in it's achievement, the jewel of Divine Love has more facets to it than the most brilliant star in the heavens. Its shining Light is our Divine Father.

The soul incarnates in many forms. May I relate to you all that the first human soul to incarnate on the planet Earth was indeed without sight, speech, hearing, smell and taste, for at that time the vibrations of this planet did not require a high enough vibration to warrant the necessity for the granting of these gifts. When it was deemed feasible and necessary the senses were granted to the incarnated soul.

Who is to say which way mankind would have been better off, to have the crutches and slow down their growth, or to endure the hardships of the absence of the senses and force man to develop the areas of his mind to achieve the levels of vibrations that so many higher cultures and societies possess at this time? Who is to say?

It took billions of years for the vibrations on this planet to rise to the level where they became compatible to house a soul at a vibration by which mankind could exist as he does today. There have been innumerable cultures and societies of lower developed forms of human life incarnated on this planet. Many of them this day incarnated on far off planets throughout the galaxies.

There are those of you within this room this night for whom this is your last span of physical existence relating to this planet. where shall you go from here? You study, you learn, you share. You seek to elevate your vibrations to become one with your Father. You Love Him enough and trust Him enough to blindly continue your search and growth, unaware of your next step. Tonight, we shall attempt to bring you a little insight into what lies ahead for you when your cycle of incarnations on this planet have been completed.

When this joyous day arrives and the soul has assumed its rightful place within the mansions of Heaven, it will serve for an indeterminate period of time as a Spiritual Master, an Ascended Master, or shall perhaps be chosen to sit at the Council of Elders and advise.

There is another galaxy, and we shall spell it for you. "Roxamila". Some of you here have spent incarnations within this galaxy and have returned to assume a series of incarnations on Earth as service. when your series of service incarnations are over you shall return to this galaxy immediately.

When the soul's vibrations have risen to the point of assimilating to the vibrations in this galaxy, it shall begin a new series of growth patterns on one of seven planets within that galaxy. The series of incarnations normally is eighty-four and will take approximately 45,000 of your years to complete. The physical form bears no relation to the form you now possess. The last third of the incarnations are totally without physical form altogether. The soul will, at that time, have developed at the conscious level the capacities for many things that seem inconceivable in your minds at this time. Dematerialization, self-transportation within moments across galaxies, manifestation of objects, instantaneous healing, regeneration of matter and many, many more.

There is within the world that awaits you, a lack of what you call karma relating to the physical plane, for that shall be completed within the confines of your present series of incarnations. All shall be Love and growth. Some of you who are at this time among the numbered children of God, have already elected at the soul level, to remain in the confines of this galaxy to serve God in various supervisory capacities, to be master of a continent, of a hemisphere, of a planet. In time, in time beyond our conception, all souls without exception shall serve in the capacity of a Creator of a Universe, shall serve in the capacity of what you refer to as a God, and shall supervise that Universe from its conception until its demise.

At this point the soul shall have acquired the absolute vibration of Divine Love and shall be with our Divine Father for all eternity.

I say to you in a few short moments what shall take untold billions of years. However, if you can understand that this total journey is indeed a journey of Love, then the whole experience shall be as a moment.

I sit here and share with you. I send my Love to you and feel your Love in return. There are tears within this heart, but they are of joy and Love. This is the message that I bring to you this night.

I Bless you for allowing me to share with you.

Questions and Answers

Now it is time for the period of questioning. We ask Stuart to act as monitor please.

Question: It has been said that Roosevelt Dam will fall apart within a two-year span and there will be great flooding. Will you please tell us where the flooding will occur?

Answer: It is our humble opinion that the dam will not fall apart. We do not believe that your engineers are that lacking in their knowledge that any major stress would not be foreseen. We do not pick up any vibrations for this disaster, for indeed it would be a disaster.

Question: Would you please explain what was meant when Moses said that mankind's self- judgment caused us to lose touch with our Father at the conscious level?

Answer: There is no one who judges mankind, except for mankind itself. Even God does not sit in judgment. Each soul creates its own truth. When a man feels that he has strayed from God's path, he has made that decision for himself. He has, therefore, created a situation which shall allow the energies of negativity to emerge. This creates the energies for new lessons to help him prove to himself that he is correct: and so, this occurred within mankind with the creation of idols and idol worship, with the leaving of God's Path and God's Laws of truth. The Law is simply stated: "When you take an action within your existence that you believe to be your truth, you are Blessed. When you take an action and know in your heart that it is not your truth, you create your own lessons."

Question: Referring to your statement that all souls will be creators of Universes. Are we not a complete Universe within ourselves and the creator of that Universe?

Answer: Most assuredly so. Each one of us is our own Universe unto ourselves. Each one of us is unto ourselves our own temple of our Father, and all is in preparation for greater things to be done.

Question: As far as my struggle to find God in myself, the more I try, the more I find my will leading me away from this path. Can you please help me?

Answer: You must sit down in truth and admit to yourself what you have done with the course of your life that causes you not to like yourself, even if it causes pain. If you will allow the energies of admittance to yourself, then it becomes easy to release and to make room for the Love vibration to re-enter your heart. Your walking of God's path is within you. The energies of your Father are in your heart. Begin to learn to Love yourself. Begin to accept yourself as you are and release the self-guilt that you have saddled yourself with over the past eight months. No one has asked you to impose this upon yourself, only you, and you have no need for it. Do you understand what we are saying to you? "Yes."

Question: Why must there be a demise of every Universe ever created? If a Universe is functioning according to God's Laws and keeps on doing so, it would seem to me that there would be no reason to terminate that Universe. Would you explain that to me please?

Answer: The creation, the building, the achieving, the declining and the end of a Universe are part of the evolutionary process of Creation. They are created to serve a Divine purpose. Even in the decline of a Universe, it serves a purpose, for it exposes souls within that Universe to lessons of growth. We must all submit ourselves to the overall total process of evolution, for at any given moment within the expanses of Creation, the existence of a Universe has ended, and the creation and emergence of a new one has taken place. It is, if you can look at it from a very broad aspect, no different from physical birth and death. It is just the normal evolutionary process on a different level.

Question: Scientists have expanded on a theory of the expansion and contraction of the Universe. Is this a physical manifestation that they are picking up on of this creation and transition of a Universe?

Answer: What they are referring to relates to the expansion and contraction of gases within the confines of the Universe which are given off from various planet through the solar systems. Any relation would be purely coincidental within this area.

Question: It has been said that the spiritual community of Phoenix and the Valley of the Sun needs unification. Have you any suggestions of what we, as individuals or as groups, can do to help in this?

Answer: The energies for Unification have been flowing to this location for several years. There has been mass resistance to accepting these vibrations due to insecurities, various ego problems and so on, within the varied organizations of this city. You shall find before the end of the year, many upheavals within many New Age groups and other types of organizations. Although they claim to truly walk as one in brotherhood, they do not practice what they preach. I will say to you, to all of you, to use the energies of Unification to reach the people and then the organizations shall fall into place. The average person has no axe to grind, he is just seeking God.

Question: At the last meeting I asked a question about the Rainbow Festival and was told that I would meet a certain individual. I was at the gathering and to my knowledge, I have not met that individual, at least not by the name given to me. I was wondering if I had met that entity and we just did not come into close contact to exchange names, or if he was under another name at that gathering?

Answer: I must say that it was a case of crossed wires, for indeed he was present. The meeting will occur in time at the Sedona area.

Question: The things you told me before about my question of learning to accept myself I know in my heart are true. I find that my heart and mind are too dark to find a first step. I don't know how to help myself as far as this is concerned.

Answer: Then we shall help you now. We ask you to rise from your chair and sit on the floor in front of us. Now please, we ask everyone in this room to send this child Love, for now her first step is to be aware of the existence of God within her, and to experience this Love. This is what I ask you all to do now. Bless you all.

that acknowledgement of the is often not a simple thing to commitment of yourself to you, and many times leaves you without anything else to hold on to, and for a moment you feel all alone: but the instant you feel that recognition and oneness, you know and realize that you have never been alone and never shall be alone. This

shall bring you peace and Love in your heart.

Question: Is it possible to know the vibratory rate of one's soul?

Answer: Your soul is vibrating at the rate of 4.75. This means that you are in line with the basic vibrations of this planet, perhaps slightly ahead. It also tells you that you have the capacity to achieve a substantial level of conscious growth.

Question: I would like to know if there is anything I am doing to impede the progress towards the conscious link with my masters. I am wondering whether I am just being impatient and things are at their proper pace, or am I throwing up obstacles in my path?

Answer: I would have to say yes to both questions. You are proceeding at a proper pace, but at the same time you have created obstacles, as do most people. Realize that conscious communication with you Spiritual Masters is a whole new area of acceptance and belief. If one commits themself to belief in this area, there is very often a doubt within his mind as to its validity. Perhaps by making this commitment he might be ridiculed by society, friends, family and most of all by self. So, when the acceptance at the soul level is recognized, then it shall come to pass.

While you may feel consciously you are ready, your soul knows from your vibrations your true reaction to this situation. Allow this concept to assimilate into your mind. Ask yourself if you are ready to accept this as part of your reality.

Question: Could you shed any light on a star or planet called Altaria? If there is such a place, has it any significance to Earth?

Answer: First of all, let me say that there certainly is a planet by the name of Altaria. It has played quite a significant role within the civilizations of Earth today.

There are many souls who came to Atlantis from Altaria, and who carry spiritual names beginning with the letters ALT. Its exact location I shall not reveal to you. You have the capacity to perceive it yourself in meditation.

Question: I would like to ask about the experiments that are being conducted on Skylab. Can you shed any light on that, whether the psychokinetic energies will help or not?

Answer: I do not feel that they will have any appreciable effects.

Question: Will there be any harm done to the people of Earth due to the falling of Skylab?

Answer: There are not any vibrations for this to happen.

Question: Did the recent experiments involving 43 radio stations throughout the world applying their energies to Skylab have any effect on the Skylab? Also, were there any side effects that affected the DC-10 which crashed several hours after this experiment was conducted?

Answer: We do not feel that the experiments run by the radio stations had any appreciable effects. Also, we do not feel any relation to the airplane crash.

Question: I was wondering if there is anything that you could tell me about my relationship with the animals, I've had close contact within my life? Are they reincarnations of souls of people I have known in other lifetimes?

Answer: We must inform you that in the process of evolutionary growth, souls do not step backwards and reincarnate at the level of animals. The animal strata is a soul level unto itself, what we will say is that there is a possibility that these animals have lived with you as animals before in past lives.

Question: The PSA jet that crashed in San Diego, there were 144 people killed and the plane's numbers added up to the number eleven. In the Chicago crash, the numbers also added up to an eleven. Is there a connection?

Answer: There is no connection at all, only coincidence. Question: How about the number 144? Was that for a specific reason?

Answer: Yes. It is a number of a symbolic group of souls that have been involved within a group karmic situation in the past. The 12 of 12 symbolizes within this particular incident, a culmination of a karmic involvement. It was a vibration of energy that had to be resolved.

Question: Was there a significance to the place where it crashed as far as a sacrificial kind of thing?

Answer: There was no connection of any kind.

Question: During the lecture you said that because we have senses, there are parts of the mind that are not used, but we would have had to use if we didn't have all of our senses. Can you give us some information on how we can unlock and use that great portion of our minds that we don't use?

Answer: You ask for the pot of gold to pour into your life. If you could place yourself in a chair and have electrodes placed upon your head to remove every bit of negativity in your mind, then it would be any easy task for you to accomplish. However, all of these built-in reactions are part of the learning process that you must go through. If it will be of any consolation, which I assume it will not be, future generations shall begin to have this awareness much earlier during their lifetimes. The parents, generation by generation, are understanding more and finding their own truths, then they encourage their children to experience Love and allow them wider freedom of expression, which has been denied for so many generations. Have patience and grow.

Question: I have a son who has spiritual visitations. The problem is that they frighten him. How can I help him?

Answer: Explain to him that he is not alone in this experience. Tell him that this experience is not abnormal. Share with him in his experiences and explain what is happening. Teach him to meditate and join him. Togetherness dissipates fear.

If there are no more questions at this time, then we shall draw this session to a close. Once again, we remind you to keep seeking other Children of Light, to help them awake, for this is the mission of us all.

We Bless you.

Chapter 12

Christos: "Alian Souls"

Good evening. This is Christos. Bless you.

We wish to speak to you this evening on a topic that has raised many questions and has caused many doubts within the minds of all. And so, we shall attempt, within the time available to us, to enlighten you and give you some understanding into the area of what is commonly known as "alien souls".

By definition, an alien soul is one that has incarnated within a society in a physical manner from a higher vibration than is presently occupying that planet. This type of incarnation is basically one of service for God, for it is not within the normal pattern of incarnation for a soul to assume an incarnation in a lower vibration.

The process to achieve this is quite complex. We cannot allow any soul to incarnate and interfere with the normal structure or patterns of societies. We cannot allow a soul to exert any abnormal influences by manifesting unusual abilities or knowledge that would alter the normal course of development within these areas. There are many alien souls within your society who could indeed solve all of your energy and other problems that confront you.

As a general rule, when an alien soul volunteers for a service incarnation for our Father, it will not be a single incarnation. It will be a series of incarnations that may span several thousand of your years. There are, of course, exceptions. There are those who, for specific purposes, will incur a single incarnation to achieve this purpose.

Reason for the long span of incarnations is to allow the soul to assimilate and adjust to the nature and character of the vibrations of those living on the planet. I did not say to readjust its vibrations. I said only to adjust to the existing vibrations on the planet. This is a very important point, for no one, not even our Father, would ask a single soul to lower its vibrations under any conditions. It is truly a matter of learning to adjust, to intermesh, and to be able to involve itself with others while maintaining its own level of vibrations.

There are, at this time, many millions of souls walking the face of this planet whose vibrations have risen past the point of balance within the vibrations of this planet, who are qualified to be called what we refer to as alien souls. A great number of those children being born within the last ten years are comprised of this category of soul, and the number shall increase as time passes. We do not have time to wait any longer.

When a soul has volunteered to assume an incarnation within a lower vibration, before it begins its service it must undergo a period of training and readjustment. It will undergo this while still in spirit form. It will be subjected to souls of the equivalent vibrations to the planet it will incarnate on. This will help it, while still in spirit form, to adapt and adjust to being involved with that degree of vibration. This process in itself takes several hundred of your years. If this were not done, the following problems would arise: There would be mass insanity and suicide by the more highly evolved soul after it had in-carnated on the planet. Its sensitivity of vibration, its inability to function within the society at that level could make it a total misfit emotionally, psychologically, intellectually and spiritually.

There are those among you in this room who have experienced these problems to some degree. Fortunately, you have received ex-planation and guidance along your path and direction, but all are not so fortunate. There are many who are lost. The result is very often quite similar to those who, upon coming into conscious realization of the Christ within, loose their concepts of reality and find them-selves incapable of handling and accepting these energies.

118

Out of the forty-one people sitting in this room, there are thirteen alien souls present at this time. This is quite a high percentage, but not high in relation to the composition of those who are present. There are drawbacks to an alien soul assuming this type of service, for indeed, the soul exposes itself to drawing to it new areas of karmic lessons, new situations to work out.

What happens when an alien soul assumes a physical incarnation and during the course of that incarnation never truly comes to conscious awareness of its true identity, for indeed this does occur. When this type of situation arises, as a general rule, we will find that the individual, at the conscious level, is involved in acts within its lifetime that tend to go to extremes, such as violence and crime, such as achieving great power through business ventures and organizations and misusing the power.

The cause of this condition is the total unacceptance, at the conscious level, of the impulses, of the feelings that the soul is imparting to it at the conscious level, the rejection of the spiritual connection. This results in consciously rebelling against the laws of God and consequently against the laws of man and society. The sensitivity of the vibration can be expressed at either end of the scale, either in love or in hate.

If an alien soul is involved within this category of incarnation, when the incarnation has ended and the soul is called to account for its accomplishments during that period of incarnation, it must show that it did its best to make the conscious being aware of its identity. If this is not so, it shall have the right to terminate its service incarnations and return whence it came. If the soul had truly made a sincere effort to achieve its purpose, it shall assume another incarnation within a fairly short period of time to resume its work on the planet.

The prime function of an alien soul is to raise its vibrations to where they emit Divine Love to all who come in contact with it, to become consciously aware of self, and to use this vibration of Love to awaken the balance of God's Children into accepting His eternal Existence. In order to achieve this at the conscious level, there is often much pain and emotional turmoil experienced within the process. It involves breaking the balance between the physical and the spiritual, releasing the emotional plane, and allowing the Love vibration to become the dominant tone, rather than the balancing one. It is at this point within a soul's growth that many Children of Light are lost for the balance of the incarnation.

There are tens of thousands of God's Children who study and work to develop their awareness consciously, who reach the point to make the decision to commit themselves to their path and to God, but cannot find the strength to break the balance, to cut the cord, to sever the knot.

We are at a time and place within the development of this planet when we can no longer sit back and wait. It is a necessity to bring your vibrations to a level of consciousness. As we have said to you before, we are rapidly approaching a point where the basic vibrations of this planet shall rise, and you must rise with them.

Many alien souls are spiritually guided and assisted in the fulfillment of their missions by our brothers and sisters circling this planet in one of the innumerable ships that have traveled here from far off worlds and civilizations to serve. Those of you who are in conscious communication with our space brothers can generally be sure they are serving you in this capacity. They shall continue to do so until you reach the point of conscious self-realization.

I say to you that it does not matter if one is an alien soul or not. We are, in the ultimate, all as one: none better, none worse. At any given moment, there is not one soul that does not have more knowledge in one area than another, and equally the opposite is true.

This is the message I bring you this night.

I Bless you for allowing me to share my truth in our Father's Name.

Questions and Answers

Now it is time for the questioning. You may proceed.

Question: I was interested in your statement that the prime objective was to manifest Divine Love. I wondered if those people like myself are stopped on streets and asked for help by strangers very frequently, who assist other people because they come to them without solicitation, are manifesting that and being recognized by other souls as ones who will indeed help them?

Answer: This is absolutely correct, and I must say to all of you that most of you are aware of this. Over your course of study and development, and as your vibrations have risen, you all have found more and more people approaching you to ask questions involving spiritual growth without any knowledge of your involvement, seeking your advice in many areas because of the acceptance of your Love vibrations, of the feeling of being comfortable within your presence and at ease with you. This will increase and grow, for it is the greatest tool we possess.

Question: Can you tell me the purpose for the vibrations of the constellation Orion?

Answer: We shall answer this question specifically in relation to you. The vibrations from this constellation do have an effect on you. They tend to guide and steer your emotional stability. It is a source of power and energy that is available for you to draw on when you feel weakened or under stress in the emotional area. It shall supply new strength and energy for these purposes. The constellation in itself is basically serving as an energy boosting station, or perhaps better said, as a relay station for energy.

Question: What time does the soul enter the body? How is the soul created originally?

Answer: To answer your question properly would take us at least four months, but we say this to you. The soul enters the body at the instant of conception, as a general rule. The exception is when specific karmic situations are involved, causing the soul to wait outside to enter the body at the first conscious breath. This will cause certain deformities within the child, either physically or mentally.

A soul is created from a single cell of energy released from the Universal energy mass, and allowed to mature, to grow and develop in isolation until it has reached maturity.

Question: In reference to alien souls, is there a way through the numerology we have learned here to identify them?

Answer: Indeed, there is. When you find a person who has within the area of seven aspects, two or more with the combinations of total ten and one, you shall know they are an alien soul.

Question: In numerology I have several with a total of one. Would I then be an alien soul?

Answer: What we are referring to is not the standard form of numerology. It is a new method of combinations of numbers that has been taught at this center.

Question: You said that the level of vibrations would be rising on this planet. What happens to the souls that have not become aware and stay at the present level of vibration?

Answer: This is what shall result in what the world is looking forward to as a holocaust, or as what they call cataclysmic changes that shall occur on Earth. These types of changes shall be more at a spiritual and conscious level than involving the physical structure of this planet. There shall be much violence. There shall be much discomfort and much unhappiness. You must understand that the course of evolution cannot be changed or altered. All are offered the same chance to grow. Those who do not wish to avail themselves, or deny the existence of their Father, shall have to stand aside or fall by the wayside. In their ensuing incarnations they shall no longer incarnate within the confines of this planet, for their vibrations will no longer be compatible with this planet.

It will either be that choice, or it shall come to a point, within centuries to come, when the lower vibrations shall truly destroy this planet and themselves along with it. In either case, those who walk with the Father shall indeed survive.

Question: The northern California entities seem to have a lot of changes taking place. Are they good changes, or not?

Answer: The vibrations within the area of which you speak have allowed themselves to be consumed by negativity, fear and doubt. They are not dwelling upon what is in their lives at this time, but what they fear may be present within an unknown future that for them does not exist, and so they take unto their vibrations some negativity, some doubt and some fear. They must learn that their tomorrow is today, that their yesterday was an hour ago, and that their reality is now, and live their lives in Love for the present. Let them use their energies to make future feelings ones of Love, not doubt and fear.

There are many areas within this country where vibrations have changed for these same reasons. When you return home, bring them these words and perhaps they can use them to realize what they are doing to their lives and futures.

Question: I have just recently read another channeling that says that the negative powers have just as much power nowadays as the positive powers, and the positive powers no longer have the control that they used to have. What is your thinking on this?

Answer: For those who believe this to be, it is. For those who believe that they walk in the Light and the good, they do. I am not saying this to avoid or to hedge on your question. I am saying this as fact. If one accepts that negativity is as powerful as Love, then it shall be.

I would say that there was a conscious injection within the energies of that channeling to indicate the feelings of insecurity that allowed the expression of this message.

Question: When an alien soul comes here after studying to be able to accept the vibrations that are here, does that alien soul still have its high intelligence?

Answer: Absolutely so. The only thing the alien soul studies is to learn to adjust to and encounter a lower vibration, to be able to achieve communication and relationship with it without allowing it to affect its own vibrations. In other words, to develop the capacity to relate to others at all levels, to make them comfortable within its vibrations even though theirs may be of a lower rate, and yet not to be affected by it, to stand apart and yet be involved.

Question: Why does the alien soul stand aside and bides time, so to speak, rather than letting it be known who he is?

Answer: You must understand that if we, who sit here and speak to you now, had declared to you who we were as recently as two years ago, you would have denied our words to you. You would have accused us of walking in ego and probably have left our vibrations, and so all can only be said when the energies of acceptance are there, when the energies of communication have been established, when understanding is present. One cannot go out and speak truth to deaf ears and closed minds.

Question: Is it permissible for an alien soul to extend itself by writing and being able to inform others how to raise their vibrations for the God Love, the being with One?

Answer: This is the basic part of the purpose of the alien soul, to help others learn to grow and to elevate their vibrations, to be aware of their true identities. My answer is yes, of course.

Question: If these alien souls come from a planet of a higher vibration, where do the non-alien souls come from?

Answer: The majority of souls incarnated on this planet at the present time have assumed a series of incarnations here as a part of their evolutionary growth. They have come here from planets and galaxies whose vibrations were lower than that of the planet Earth. When they had, within the planet or galaxy, raised their vibrations past the point of that existing planet, it was time for them to incarnate on a planet of higher vibration as a part of their normal growth process. There are certain areas within the karmic pattern of learning that are native to this planet and to its societies. For these reasons, the majority of souls are here as part of their evolutionary growth and development.

Question: Would you say that the alien souls, as opposed to coming in the normal pattern of growth, are coming here with specific missions to help mankind?

Answer: That is exactly correct.

Question: I have heard you speak prior to tonight of this being the last incarnation of a particular soul. What happens then?

Answer: When a soul finishes its pattern of incarnation related to this planet, it serves in spirit form, usually in the capacity of a guide or Master, to assist other souls still within their pattern of physical incarnation. It may assume a position on any one of an innumerable number of advisory boards. It may volunteer to return to Earth on a specific mission for God. When its vibrations have reached the point that is what we call optimum, it will then move into other galaxies, other Universes or worlds to continue to grow in areas and levels of development beyond your comprehension. This process will continue until the soul shall be a manifestation of total Divine Love. Then it shall reassimilate and become one with our Divine Father.

Question: I can't help feeling that I have a special purpose and mission. Do you have any message for me this night?

Answer: You do indeed have a special purpose and mission, as do all who are sitting within this room, so my answer is for all to hear. It is not yet time for us to make you aware of your true spiritual purpose at this time. You must grow into the readiness; you must grow into the acceptance of what awaits you. Continue your growth. You shall, within a short period of time, be told spiritually of the first step that your path shall take you upon. This information must come to you from your own spiritual teachers and Masters. They are in charge and care of your growth. It would not be proper for me to interfere with their assigned positions in your life.

Question: In your comments you said that one of our tasks was to use the vibration of Love, not as a balance point but as the dominant energy. How does one do that?

Answer: When you reach the point within your spiritual growth that you can say to yourself that you recognize, accept and feel the energies of the Chirst within you, then it shall all have come to pass. These are the energies of Love. The experiencing of the Christ consciousness is comparable to receiving your Ph.D. At that point you may accept it or reject it. You may have the ability to handle it, or you may not.

126

Question: In recent weeks I have been suffering a lot of injuries in the physical body, all of them in the left side in various joints. I have not had too much success in eliminating them. I was wondering if you could offer any suggestions?

Answer: We suggest that you have your mate rebalance the flow of energies throughout your body on a daily basis. Because of the type of strenuous activity that you participate in during the course of the day, you are creating this imbalance of flow within your body. This results in the susceptibility to weakness, sore muscles, etc., within your body.

Question: Is it possible for an alien soul to be awakened or enlightened and fulfill most of its mission without being in conscious communication?

Answer: It is possible, but not probable. The reason for that is that the knowledge available to one with normal consciousness and normal intellectual pursuits is far below the degree of information and awareness that is available at the level of communication with self. It is possible to achieve much just through the Love vibration, but to pursue a mission, to serve in the capacity of a teacher, a counselor or advisor, usually necessitates the availability of the higher truths of self. You must understand that this level of communication comes to all at varying times and degrees. There is no set pattern for consciousness.

Question: Isn't it true that we live in spirit and in the physical at the same time, and that we need to learn what we are really doing?

Answer: Let me phrase it another way. I am Christos, the soul of the conscious being, Frank. I am Spirit, as I have always been. He is a conscious expression of My existence. He is here to be the tool, the method for Me to consciously achieve My purposes for this incarnation. He has accepted Me totally and We are one in expression, so what you have said is true, but it is only true where there has been total acceptance between the physical expression and the soul or Spirit.

Question: I feel that there is a constant vibration between the soul of me and the conscious expression of me. It is like an up and down vibration just going on between the two parts of the whole. Is that a correct feeling?

Answer: That is absolutely correct.

Question: I wonder if you could give me your thoughts and views about LSD and other hallucinogenic drugs as to their true uses, advantages, disadvantages and the method of action upon the soul?

Answer: In my truth, the use of any alien type of substance to achieve illumination or enlightenment shall lead you to only darkness. For one who is not consciously involved, to me, it does not matter, for he is using his own free will. For one who is involved and growing, who knows that such things are improper for his vibrations, he shall find that he shall achieve some growth and stop. Then his growth shall slowly leave him. There comes a point of no return, and he shall fall by the side.

We must now draw this session to a close. We Bless you all for allowing us to share our energies and our truth this night.

We Bless you in our Father's Name.

Chapter 13

Blossom channeling Solomon

Good evening my children. I would like to welcome you and Bless you this night, to tell you how important it is for you to be here this night. This is a very important time for growth. I am here to deliver a message. As for who I am, I sit very close to the Father. He has asked me to deliver this message to you. It is to learn, my children, help others, find others to find God. Search out within yourself for your higher self, for the God within you. There is so much for me to impart to you. I shall talk to you in your meditations. I must leave you now. Bless you.

Christos

Good evening, this is Christos. Bless you.

I am sure most of you are slightly surprised at the special offering that Blossom has just presented this night. It was requested earlier that we allow this to occur, for her growth as well as for yours.

We are pleased to share our words and our vibrations with those of you who have not graced this circle before, and we welcome you.

Tonight, we wish to discuss with you the adjustment problems that face the alien soul incarnated physically on the planet Earth, the problems that the soul faces within physical society as well as within its spiritual growth and conscious awakening to its responsibilities. We did not have the opportunity last month to complete our lecture on this topic, so we shall complete it tonight.

For those of you who have not heard our word, we define an alien soul as one who has incarnated on the planet Earth from a higher vibration and is here to do service for God, to help those incarnated on this planet find the God within themselves and continue to elevate their own vibrations.

The Law of Cause and Effect plays a heavy role in relation to the alien soul here on Earth. We have previously discussed the sensitivity of the vibrations, and very often the incompatibility with the vibrations of those seeking their growth incarnated on Earth. Each soul always has two choices, the active or passive expression. The sensitivity of vibration could cause the individual to buckle and crumble and fall by the wayside. It could consider itself incapable of forming normal relationships with people due to its sensitive nature. Conversely, it could search within itself and seek and find those with whom it can share a love and compatibility, accepting the difference within their personalities, within their structure, and within their purposes during the course of their lifetime.

This is not easy to do. The majority of us do not like to feel that we are different. We do not like to feel that we may be manifesting an ego situation, considering ourselves better than our fellow man. In truth, this is not the case.

There is no one better than any other. The acceptance must be there. The knowledge and understanding that you are here to teach, that you are here to relate to those whose development has not yet reached the conscious expression, whose vibrations have not reached the level of yours consciously, is the purpose for you being here. You must accept your role humbly and with humility.

A teacher must allow himself to be called a teacher. A student who wishes to call his teacher a guru must be allowed to do so, for this is the student's need at that particular time. We all preach to accept ourselves as we are, to admit the different facets of our personality and structure are present, to love ourselves in total acceptance. Why then should one deny this acceptance, if one has reached a higher level of growth and has an obligation to use that growth for the benefit of others? Too many times the teacher hides behind a cloak or shield and will not stand upon the stage behind the podium and says, "At this time, for however long you have a need, I am here to offer my services, my energies and my Love to you, for your understanding and your growth."

At times we find an individual of a higher vibration who feels that it is impossible for him to pursue a normal job situation, or to pursue normal social relationships with

others within the community or the structure of society, and so I will explain to you the role that one must assume under these circumstances.

It is never requested of any individual to lower his vibrations in order to relate to another individual, yet the capacity to relate to others must be totally universal. This is achieved by permitting the relationship without involvement, serving in the capacity that is necessary for you to serve in. Emit your Love vibration to all those around you, help them grow and understand and yet, stand alone. In this manner you shall not become drained or subjected to negativity. This is part of the meaning of what I have said to you so long ago, that when one walks the Path of God, that when one makes the commitment to do God's work, one must also accept that he walks alone.

The alien soul, in spite of the fact of the spiritual level of its vibrations, or perhaps I should say because of the fact of its spiritual vibrations, is often subjected to a greater amount of negativity than the average person. His sensitivity creates a vulnerability. If he is not consciously aware of the nature of his vibrations, he may never totally achieve his mission in life. For this reason, I ask you all in your travels and in your search for other Children of Light, to be sensitive to those who seem to be lost. They seem to be living in a world of their own, walking with their heads in the clouds. They need assistance and must learn to be grounded.

All those who are physically incarnated are here to be involved within the physical as well as the spiritual, or they would not be here. The prime mission of every soul, regardless of what stage of development he is at, is for his own growth then to assist others in their growth. Everything else is secondary. This is why we must not isolate ourselves from any segment of the population. We cannot become too sensitive to be involved with those performing within the physical structures of society. Never, never forget that the poor soul that you see lying in the gutter, drunk beyond all reason, may be a Spiritual Master. Always bear that in your mind.

There are at this time, and shall be in greatly increasing numbers for many, many years to come, highly developed souls and Masters incarnating on this planet. The children of today and those of tomorrow and many tomorrows, shall be aware to a far greater degree than we expect. Most of them shall fall into this category of what we have termed alien souls, truly not alien, but just of a higher more developed vibration. Those of you who shall bear children, hear my words and be aware to allow your children, from the moment of their first breath, to be smothered in nothing but Love. This will create a dominance of the Love vibration in their reaction patterns. It will allow them the expression of their minds and their directions. Guide them and steer them. Do not stifle their minds, their explorations and their sensitivities, for they are the ones that shall change the world. They are the ones that shall bring us all together under God.

The path of spiritual evolvement begins as a superhighway with four, six or eight lanes. As we travel down this highway, we are permitted to change lanes as often as we wish. We move to a lane of slower traffic, or pass cars, or pull off at one of the exits. The longer the road continues, the narrower it becomes. When one has reached the point within his growth and development that he has recognized the vibrations of our Father within himself, has acknowledged His presence and committed himself to his path, the highway becomes a single lane road. It becomes narrower and narrower. Soon one must take leave of the vehicle and walk until one is confined so that he must place one foot in front of the other to stay on the path. At that time, one is truly walking alone, and yet never alone. Our Father is always with us.

Sensitivity is not a sign of weakness; it needs assistance in finding its direction and its place. Be aware of your vibrations. Be aware of your capacities and your abilities. If you have difficulty relating to a situation within your life, do not act rashly. Seek advice from one of your brothers or sisters. All are here to assist one another for we are all, indeed, as one.

Questions and Answers

These are the words that I share with you this night. Now it is time for the questioning period. We ask Stuart to act as monitor and we Bless you in our Father's Name.

Question: Do alien beings reincarnate the same as non-alien beings through different families, or do they go through the same family?

Answer: When an alien soul volunteers for a service mission for our Father it is rarely for one or two incarnations alone. Normally he must involve himself within the total pattern of incarnation assigned to the particular planet. He must abide by all the rules of incarnation that are assigned to that planet, so I would say that the rules of incarnation are no different than the rules for any other soul with one exception: the vehicle to carry the birth of the child must be of a higher vibration in order to avoid miscarriage and insure the proper birth.

Question: Would you please explain impersonal Love versus personal Love, out of body projection, and the goals of man? How they relate?

Answer: Our definition of impersonal Love is expressed in the following manner. We Love you as a soul. We Love you as a child of God. We Love you because you are a brother and we are as one and yet, the personal involvement or personal Love I do not share with you. I am not a part of the conscious personality of your emotions. I am not involved with your reactions, nor you with mine. Therefore, as a conscious being, my personal Love has not been extended to you at this time, yet I Love you.

What is known as out of body experiences shall occur to all from time to time. Many of you consider them dreams and that is fine. I would not overly accent or stress this type of occurrence, as I place it in a class of phenomena. If you achieve this ability at a conscious level for growth and to project yourself into the energies of another time and place for information, then it is a benefit for you. To use it as a game, as a thing of exploration without purpose, is quite unnecessary.

Question: Has the prophesized battle of Armageddon already taken place and been won by the forces of Light on the inner planes?

Answer: The battle of Armageddon is expressed in two areas. There is a battle occurring within the physical plane spiritually as well as in the others. It has not come to a conclusion at either end, but it shall come to a conclusion, a conclusion for Love and Light as there is no greater force. The turmoil that is expressed within the confines of this planet in the mind of man shall increase in intensity. As more and more Children of Light become aware of their identities, as more people raise their spiritual vibrations, those who have not chosen to do so shall become uncomfortable within the Love and the knowledge. This too, is a facet of Armageddon.

Question: Would you explain, define and elaborate on vibrations?

Answer: A vibration is the oscillation of a beam of energy. The more at peace and the less variation within the oscillation, the more spiritual becomes the vibration. All energy travels and is used by means of vibration. The closer we come to being with our Divine Father, the smoother becomes the vibration. Think of those you know whom you consider to be spiritually evolved. Think how peaceful they are, how in a normal situation that would agitate or excite another individual, they are able to cope without losing control of their peace and calmness. This is part of our purpose for growth, for when our vibrations have increased to the point where movement is hardly noticed, the heat is absent due to the lack of intensity, then we have come closer in our search for Divine Love.

Question: Would you explain to me the sounds or words that are heard on the higher planes, the higher vibrations?

Answer: Basically, these sounds are the vibrations from energy that is coming to you, to energize you, to teach you, to raise your vibrations. It is rather difficult to categorize the sound within the specific nature of a note, or a specific tune, for they come to each of us in different degrees. You must understand that within a single color there are thousands of variations of intensity and vibration. There are many civilizations within the Universe who communicate with light and sound according to different intensities and degrees of vibration. Therefore, they exist without the necessity of physical speech such as you on Earth are confined to.

Question: A few months ago, a woman asked you to pinpoint her vibration orientation number. You told her it was four point something. Does the figure you gave her correlate to the twelve planes of Earth?

Answer: I believe that we mentioned to her that her vibrations were operating on a scale of 4.75. I was not relating to the twelve levels or planes. I merely was relating it to the level of vibrations that is most common on the surface of this planet at this time. I do not like to, nor do I wish to categorize or place different people on any sort of scale of achievement, for that would be of limiting nature and scope.

Question: Is Solomon always right?

Answer: I would hate to admit what he would do to me if I denied that. It depends from whose point of view you are speaking. To quote in his own words: "I am the Silver Fox, I never lie. I do many things that I call negative truth." All he does for you is for your growth. He may seem quite stern at times, but in the long analysis all is done with total Love and for your growth. Understand that his position is to remain detached from his initiates. His job is most difficult, but quite rewarding.

Question: Is it possible to consciously and visually recognize an alien soul? How?

Answer: Absolutely so. What I say is of a general nature and not specific, for there are always exceptions. Within the Caucasian race their eyes shall be hues that are pale hazel, blue, green and grey. Their complexions shall be fair. They often appear to be as dreamers and prefer to spend much time by themselves. These are the basic superficial characteristics. If you have the ability to recognize different levels of vibrations, you will have no difficulty recognizing them just from their energies. They exude great Love. This is not to say that there are not alien souls who have black or brown hair and eyes and olive skin. I am only speaking generally.

Question: Is it possible to raise your vibrations to those that you describe as an alien soul through conscious means, or does one have to incarnate as an alien soul?

Answer: The main purpose of every incarnation we assume is to consistently raise our vibrations. That is mankind's prime function. We achieve this through conscious growth. It certainly is possible and most desirable for everyone to do so. This is basically achieved through meditation. Without meditation, I would say as a general rule, it cannot be achieved. You must put yourself within the vibrations and the presence of God to allow His Energies to flow to you to raise your vibrations.

The more you share your Love with others, the more it returns to you tenfold. To achieve growth and keep it for yourself is a waste and will serve you no purpose. Share and receive in return.

Question: Who is Solomon, and what does he do?

Answer: Solomon is the name of the soul that walked this plane as Solomon, the son of King David. The true name of his soul is not Solomon. He uses that name to allow us to recognize him in perhaps his most famous incarnation here on Earth. This helps us to understand his position, his level of development and his wisdom. The true name of the soul of Solomon is Urantia. He sits at the Hand of God and is responsible for the planet Earth in the area of teaching those children who have committed themselves to the Path of God. He guides them through their initiations and assists them on their roads to achieving mastery in their current incarnations. That is part of who Solomon is.

Question: Last Tuesday we were visited by a spirit by the name of Nehi Chinn. I am curious because some saw the spirit, and some did not. My question is why that even though I feel that some were more knowledgeable than I, they did not see him? Were they not open? What helps you to be able to see this form?

Answer: It is important that all of you understand that each one of you expresses your knowledge and growth in different areas. No two of you shall totally experience the same things. Some shall see auras with the naked eye, some shall not, and so on. Each of us is responsible unto ourselves. Never compare yourself or your growth to another person. The other person may not have the same mission, the same path, the same lessons to learn. It is not a lack of growth not to have seen Nehi Chinn, only a phase of growth as yet undeveloped. All must accept their own abilities without questioning why, or why not. All receive what they have earned and what will help them achieve their purpose in life. They are tools for you to use to help others become aware of the presence of God. They have no other purpose.

Question: I read a book on Tibetan Buddhism that gave a technique of meditation where a person sits in lotus position staring into a mirror, and at a certain point he can't see himself anymore, he disappears. Is that achieving a higher vibration?

Answer: Truly not. If you were to go home and sit in front of your mirror with a dim light approximately six feet behind you, stare at a fixed point on your face, your face would disappear from the mirror. It has nothing to do with spiritual growth or evolvement. You are building an energy field between yourself and the image in the mirror that will blank out the image.

Question: What is the destiny of the Phoenix Light Center as far as transmission of spiritual energies is concerned?

Answer: The Phoenix area is indeed one of beautiful spiritual vibrations. It shall continue to grow and to flourish as long as those that are here nourish it. In other words, I truly cannot answer your question, for there is too much free will involved that could alter the vibrations in your city. There are many areas in California where the spiritual vibrations have all but been destroyed. Many of those who are highly evolved are moving to Phoenix for this reason. It is up to those living here to insure and protect their vibrations.

Question: Just recently, the scientists have been inferring that one of the moons of either Jupiter or Saturn can support life as we know it on this planet. Could this, by any chance, be the planetary body that is to be used for holding over those souls that do not grow and develop?

Answer: No. This is not so.

And now we bring this session for this month to a close. We ask you to please remember to be aware of your brothers and sisters, to seek out and find other Children of Light and expose them to any of the variety of centers of Light and learning, that they too may begin to walk their path and begin their growth. While you are waiting to find your mission for God this is your mission. Bless you for sharing your presence and your energies with us this night.

In the Name of our Divine Father, I Bless you all.

Chapter 14

Christ Spirit on Spiritual Growth

I Bless you this night with the energies of the Divine Spirit. The words that you are hearing at this time are through the energies of the Christ Spirit.

We have not spoken to you in this manner for many months, for there has been total unity within this soul. Periodically we shall isolate ourselves to bring you a message that pertains particularly to our specific vibrations.

There are many of you here this night that are in need of extra Love, of extra healing and of extra strength at this time. So, I ask you to please raise your hands above your heads with your palms up. Close your eyes and be ready to receive Our Love and healing energies.

(A long silence.)

It is done.

I have chosen to say a few words to you this night as it is important for your growth for you to understand exactly what is occurring in your lives at this time. There are too many of the Divine Spirit's children who are growing, reaching for a level, achieving that level, and becoming satisfied to remain there. They feel that they have achieved their purpose, have reached their awakening and are fulfilled.

We are losing too many who are locking themselves into the psychic vibrations and not making their transition into the spiritual realms. As you traverse through the different levels of consciousness in your search for fulfillment always remember that each stage or level you attain is merely a learning experience, or a stop on the way to total assimilation on the highest level. Keep stretching, yearning and seeking for that oneness within the vibrations of your soul. Only then will you truly find love and peace.

The vibrations are increasing in quality and intensity. Your growth will occur at a much-increased pace. Be aware that those who do not grow, or who at this time have not lit the candles of Light which burn in them, will express the balancing negative energies and will need your assistance. Never forget that you are here to learn to be Love, then to teach that Love to others, to allow them to feel it and have it flow through their vibrations. Always keep searching for more, never rest. Never feel that you have achieved what you are here to achieve, for there shall always be more. Always there will be more. I Bless you all this night.

Christos: The Relationship of Soul to Spirit

This is Christos, and I Bless you.

We are going to talk to you tonight about the relationship of soul to Spirit. A friend of ours, one called Nehi Chinn, or in our frame of reference, Nahi Chinn, has opened a door and stimulated some questions in this area. With this in mind we shall try to expand and expound on these energies.

Within the realm of God, within the realm of Divine Spirit, all is Spirit. If all is Spirit, then all is soul. However, if all is soul, all is not truly in the real sense of the word, Spirit. All soul is part of Spirit. Each energy force that is a child of the Divine Spirit carries with it, and manifests from it, an umbrella of energies. This umbrella is similar to the one you are sharing, feeling, and experiencing this evening and partake of when you come to this sanctuary to learn and to grow. The energies under this umbrella are available to you even when you are not physically present here. Once the link has been made and the desire for growth has been established, all facets of these energies are available to assist you, aid you in your growth, protect, love and comfort you. So, it is throughout the Universe.

We sit here as Spirit. Under the umbrella of our energies there are twelve souls. Under the umbrella of the energies of all Spirit there are twelve souls or divisions. Each one is a part, an integral part that goes to make up the composition of the Spirit. This is indeed the twelve of twelve. This is why, when the Spirit of Christ walked with Jesus, there were twelve disciples. Each one was a facet, a soul related to and carrying the vibrations and the energies of the Christ Spirit.

There will be untold thousands of circles of twelve created on the physical plane. This is how we shall return the Children to the Divine Spirit. Each one of the twelve is a part of the whole. Each one carries every facet of the energies of the construction and composition of the Spirit. And so, when one soul under an umbrella consciously meets another soul of the same umbrella, there is instantaneous Love. There is compatibility. There is recognition. Many people consider this a meeting of soul mates. Perhaps, in a way, this is true.

This structure has been set up for very definite purposes. If there is an extremely important mission for the family of souls to achieve as a unit, then the Core of the Spirit will also incarnate. The souls in the family group will be drawn to the Core of the Spirit to assimilate the knowledge. This may occur unconsciously, but it will occur. All must share the same Love. All must share the same purpose and the same dedication to their path. Each one is aware of the feelings of the others.

The twelve souls do not always incarnate at the same time. They may have different missions. The only time all twelve incarnate together is for a special mission for which the Spirit Core also incarnates.

When a physical incarnation is completed, the soul, upon making its transition, remains independent of the Spirit. With the help of the Spirit, the soul assesses the knowledge acquired during the incarnation and determines its next incarnation. In the end, when there is no longer a need for additional incarnations, all twelve souls assimilate with the Spirit Core to become as One. The Spirit will leave the vibrations of this solar system and, perhaps, the Universe, to begin another higher level of growth and service for the Divine Spirit.

There are many whom mankind refers to as Elevated Masters or Ascended Masters. They have assimilated and become Spirit totally, giving them the knowledge, learning and experiences of all the facets that have been split away for all of those incarnations. There are some Spirit Cores within this circle tonight.

I want you to understand that part of the reason we share this with you this night is for you to be aware that there are others that you shall meet who will become as one with you, that no matter how many times you feel you walk the path alone, you are never alone. Like energies will be drawn to you when the time comes for you to begin working toward the completion of your mission and toward the end and finality of your destiny.

The energies for many missions have been formulated and are within the ethers: the astral and Earth vibrations waiting for those who grow to have the capacity to tune in and accept these missions as their own. We have been teaching you recently to rise above the level of the psychic vibrations, to reach toward Spirit, to raise yourself higher and higher. Pursue this endeavor even though it may take some time, and you may seem to be walking alone in darkness. You are not. Consider it a test of your durability and strength in your beliefs. When you reach the Light, the rewards shall be outstanding.

These are the words I share with you this night.

Questions and Answers

Now we may proceed with the questioning.

Question: Could you explain more about the function of the full moon and how it affects us?

Answer: When the moon is full, one half of its total surface is exposed to the light and energies from the sun. This gives it immense reflective and refractive power of light and energy to this planet, as well as to others. It is as if one was touched with a wire containing 40 volts of electricity and became comfortable with that. Then, one day a month, was touched with a wire containing 100 volts of electricity. It would be a shock to the system or a surge of energy that comes to you.

Those who through their growth walk with their vibrations at a higher level, are capable of handling this increased energy without disturbing their vibrations. In fact, it works as a healing and a stimulant for their energies. Those who do not have the capability of handling this level of energy suffer in turmoil, despair, despondency and a feeling of insecurity, for they are not able to handle what is flowing through them. This causes negative conscious reactions.

Question: Could you give us any information on the Roosevelt Dam?

Answer: We have discussed this several months ago, but we shall mention it again for you. We do not feel, at this time, that the dam is in any danger. We do not feel that there will be mass loss of life by the cracking and failure of this dam. One must understand that when words are imparted by Spirit at the conscious level they must be handled with discretion, discrimination and common sense. Many times, things are said in the form of a lesson. Spirit wants to see if the one receiving the message is sitting in the capacity of a fool, absorbing every single word, or will use their intelligence to discern truth before they relate it to others.

Question: Could you explain the term soul mates and how they differ from the soul groups that you were discussing?

Answer: In the purest essence, when two Spirits are created at the exact same instant, vibration, and location, they would be what you call "identical twins". This is when we would use the term soul mates. The chances of this occurring are quadrillions to one.

There are many whose only conscious aim in life is to find their soul mate. They feel that in this way they may reach eternal happiness. They are looking for a pipe dream. Happiness is created, not found standing on the street corner waiting for someone.

Question: Could you speak concerning the present status of the so-called "Illuminati Conspiracy"? Could you speak concerning reports from many sources both metaphysical and non-metaphysical attuned, that the officials in our country and in several others are being replaced by more light inclined doubles?

Answer: The "Illuminati" is a group of souls, which over the centuries has had the goal of dominating this plane. There are, of course, many of these forces of negativity.

There has been a withdrawal of many ships from the Earth plane at this time in case some of you have noticed the absence of activity. There has been a renewed effort on the part of the forces of negativity that needed additional assistance to overcome and surpress it. There shall always be negativity. There shall always be negative forces trying to assume control, but they shall never win. There is no greater force within Creation than the force of Love. It will always reign supreme.

In answer to your second question relating to doubles standing in for officials of government, I would relate that to a "Buck Rogers" mystery. In my truth, there is no truth to that at all. It is one of the examples of transmission from Spirit that requires great discernment and understanding. We do feel that many of the men within the power structure of government are not the same as when they took office. Certain energies have been added to the banks of their souls to move them in more positive, complete directions. This has been done, but a total removal and replacement shall not occur.

Question: Do we meet these other twelve souls from our soul group in a group all together, or perhaps have we met some in our lifetime up to this point and will meet others as we go along?

Answer: I will have to say yes to all of your questions. For indeed, you have met some. Some will be in groups, but by and large it shall be on an individual one-to-one basis for the first meeting. Then there shall be an assimilation into a group or circle. When one who is a soul of an umbrella of Spirit becomes consciously aware of the identity of the Core of the umbrella, they will be drawn to those energies and begin to share of them and learn from them. This is how the process generally occurs.

Question: Are you saying in essence then, there will be groups of twelve similar to Jesus and his disciples when the members of the group know what their mission is?

Answer: This is quite true. It is not always necessary for all twelve to be involved within the same mission, vibrations, or location within the same incarnation. It is possible that each would be assigned a different mission and perhaps, within the course of a single incarnation never truly come in contact with each other. It is only when the Core has incarnated for an extremely high-level, important mission that requires all of the twelve souls of Spirit to assist it, that all twelve shall totally work as one on the specific mission.

Question: Then there would be thirteen conscious entities?

Answer: Yes, the Spirit Core and the twelve souls

Question: Does that mean that all of the twelve souls do not have to end their incarnations at the same time?

Answer: That is quite true. When all of the twelve finally end their cycles of incarnations and are assimilated with the Spirit Core, the Spirit will then leave this Universe and continue its growth in a higher plane. It never divides again for its work will necessitate all of its knowledge and component parts.

Question: Can you tell me when or if Atlantis will rise in the next five years? If so, what will be the mission of the many to assist?

Answer: It is impossible for me to give you a specific year or time when Atlantis will resurface. There are too many variables within the vibrations of this planet. However, we shall say to you that it probably will rise by the year 2,000 A.D. The mission of those who are to assist within this area varies so greatly that I cannot relate it to you. Let me say this. All those who will be involved within this project will be informed well in advance for the role they are expected to play to allow them to prepare themselves adequately for this event. As the time approaches the date will come forth.

Question: Someone has seen the docking of a large ship on the Yuma desert. It is supposed to be eight miles long. Do you know anything about this?

Answer: The ship in question does exist. It is not quite eight miles long, more in the area of four miles long, which is quite long enough. It does exist within another dimension, or shall we say, vortex, which keeps it from being visible within the Earth's vibrations. It will remain there for a while. My suggestion would be not to go searching for it.

Remember the search to Sedona and judge yourselves accordingly. Do not fall prey once again to false communications and desires.

Question: Can you tell me what way you would recommend for a person to develop greater self-confidence?

Answer: We would ask you to rise in the morning and do a very foolish thing. Go over to the mirror, look in it and just say, "I love you." The first few days you will probably laugh from embarrassment, but after a while you will begin to believe it, and then it will become your truth. A lack of self-confidence is a lack of self-love. They are one and the same. Begin to do a self-analysis to understand what makes you operate, and to understand the different facets and reactions within your personality. Those you do not like, release and replace them with ones that are more positive. Then use them. This is the best method we can suggest to achieve self-love and acceptance.

Question: Should I continue with the writing that I have been doing? Are the ones I have received valid?

Answer: The writing you have received are essentially valid. Perhaps the time structure relating to the messages you have received is not totally accurate. There have been some instances where things have been related to you to test your sense of discrimination. That will continue to happen. Before three months have elapsed, we would like you to begin to break away from this form of communication and start to use your own mind to receive the impressions and thoughts rather than serving as a channel in the manner you are doing now. We caution you not to become implanted within a rut. We understand that it is comfortable to be where you are, but you must learn to release the crutch and take that step forward.

Question: A number of weeks ago in the desert, a falling star lit up the area all around me. I asked if I was being observed, and if so, could I see who was doing the observing. Immediately in the area of my gaze, three ships came out of the north in triangular formation and flew directly overhead. There was a surge of energy. Was this just a getting acquainted demonstration of things to come? Who was the captain of the ship?

Answer: It was indeed a "getting acquainted", as you put it, more of a recognition of your communication and thoughts: like saying, we have heard you, and we acknowledge. It is a beginning of what shall occur again. The ships were from a fleet from Venus. The name of the captain of the command ship is spelled Xarlani.

Question: How serious is the threat of Soviet troops in Cuba? If it is a threat, what should we be doing about it?

Answer: We do not believe it is a threat at this time. It is more in the capacity of an irritation that could in time become a thorn in the side. I do not believe any action will be taken at this time due to the fact that an election year is on the horizon. However, when the elections have been decided, I believe there will be more pressures exerted to remove these forces from that vicinity. There will be major objections, but I do not believe it will lead to any confrontation. It will be resolved peacefully by the removal of the troops, probably in the year 1981.

Question: I wonder how far the spirit guides influence our thoughts, both good and bad? Also, how much do bad spirits influence criminals?

Answer: Spirit attempts to influence many of our thoughts, expressed both positively and negatively. The effect of the influence really depends upon the acceptance of the thought within the conscious mind. If the individual accepts all thought, feeling that it has come from Spirit, therefore it must be gospel or total truth, then they are opening the door for a greater expression of negative thoughts and information, for they are relinquishing their control.

We do not suggest that you shut off the thought patterns. Allow them to remain loose and free, but do not act upon a thought until you have reasoned with it and feel that it is something that you agree with and seems sensible to you. Always bear in mind that this is your life. It is your final decision to take a course of action that you feel is proper and comfortable for you.

Question: Recently I had a precognitive dream and was brought into the year 1989. I was told that something important was to happen in that year. Can you elaborate on that?

Answer: The precognitive dream was for your consciousness. We will not elaborate on it further. Expansion of it must come to your own consciousness. Then it will be your decision as to the feasibility of sharing it with others. It will be your responsibility in this area of information. We shall not do your work for you.

Question: Is there a certain stage of our development when we learn what our mission is, or does it come to different people at different times during their development?

Answer: There is a definite stage of your development when you are made aware of your mission. It does come at different times for different souls. You will not be made aware of your mission until it has been determined that at the conscious level, you are totally committed to your spiritual path beyond all doubts a thousand times over. When you have contracted to take upon yourself a mission for God, there are certain spiritual gifts and abilities that are bestowed upon you. Spirit must be sure that these gifts and abilities will not be misused, that you will not become disgusted and leave your path. You will not be made aware of your path until this has been determined.

Question: I find myself in an isolated position at this time. Is there anything I can be taking advantage of to help this?

Answer: You must understand that all, during the course of development, reach what is known as a plateau. This is a time for assimilation, for acceptance, for utilizing and using the energies and growth that has come up to that point. Do not feel that you are not growing, for this is not true. Growth is constant. It never ceases. At this point it is occurring at the subconscious level. This knowledge will slowly be released to the conscious mind when the time is proper.

You are at a point in your life where you must make a decision. This is why you are in this pattern. You are going to have to decide to change the course of your life drastically. You have to decide if you are going to walk your spiritual path and do your life's work, or that you still have things to accomplish within the physical vibration. When you have made this decision, the holding pattern will stop, and your conscious growth shall resume.

Question: In the last three months I have developed three very pronounced spiritual abilities in order to help others upon the path. I feel there are more to come. Could you possibly expand on this?

Answer: I am sorry, we could, but we shall not. You must understand that your growth will come to you, and you must learn from it as you experience it. It is as if you were to say, "Christos, please tell me what is going to happen to me every day for the next year." If I were to do that, you would not achieve any growth for that whole year. I would be depriving you of the experiences of every day. This is true of your growth. To prepare you ahead of time for a lesson, eliminates the lesson. However, you are in you next to last incarnation on this plane. You will begin to go through a series of testing for your seventh and eighth levels of initiation within the next six months. It will take a year and a half to complete. Then your mission will be revealed to you.

Question: Why, over the past few years, have I been so drawn to the mountains? Am I too impatient with my spiritual growth?

Answer: I have never yet met anyone who is not too impatient with their spiritual growth.

There is, of course, a draw for all to the mountains. The higher we go, the higher the vibrations become. Even if it is only several thousand feet, we sense more of a closeness with the Divine Spirit. The air is fresher. It is quieter. The vibrations are purer.

If you had become consciously aware at birth, and growth was a normal thing for you, the impatience would not be there.

Chapter 15

This is Christos. Good evening and God Bless you.

We are indeed honored this night to have the energies of a special guest to pass a few moments with us and share with us a few truths, and perhaps enlighten our understanding of our consciousness and our being and purposes. If we shall be patient for a few moments, He shall begin.

The Spirit of Christ: Christ-Consciousness

I bring you the Blessings of the Divine Creator. I speak to you with the energies of the Spirit of Christ.

I have come to you this night for a very special purpose, to help you understand that each and every one of you is, indeed, your Father's favorite child. That each and every one of you is no lesser, no greater than the other.

It has been said throughout the ages that the time shall come again when I, in total soul, shall incarnate and walk the face of the planet Earth to bring the flock back to our Father. I say to you this night that this shall not come to pass. Although two thousand years have elapsed, humanity has not reached the point in consciousness where it would accept the teachings and words of one man. All would be exactly as it was before, and so within each soul that walks the face of your planet, has been implanted the energies of my soul, the Christ Light, to burn in each Child. In this method shall humanity at last unite, await and return to the Divine Being.

You must understand that the terminology so often used in your classes, in lectures and books does not apply in relation to my vibrations. Each incarnated being has the capacity and the ability to walk in Christ consciousness, to recognize and accept the vibrations within their heart, to become a conscious Child of Light. All that is needed to achieve this is the belief that you have the capability to do so, the desire to grow far beyond what you feel you can grow, to apply yourself diligently to overcome the obstacles that shall be laid in your path to achieving this consciousness.

There are none who are better than any other. There are some who are more dedicated, who persevere, who are not satisfied when a level of growth is reached that this is the apex of their evolvement, but strive on further and further, never resting, never becoming satisfied. Only in this manner will you awaken and become one with the Light. This is the overall mission of all mankind, for all to become Love, for as you have been told before, my energies represent the Love vibration of the one called Anoygin, who has created this Universe.

Allow the energies, as I speak, to flow to you. Experience them. I tell you that you can reach the point where what you are experiencing now you can experience twenty-four hours a day for the rest of your life. Let this be your goal, your aim, for in doing so all others who walk with you shall feel your Love, and it shall be a stimulus for them to become aware of their own.

The Messiah has returned, but not as one, as all humanity, for this is how it must be. It has been determined that only in this way can we be successful in awakening God's children. I Bless all of you. I send you our Creator's Love and energy and may you walk in Love for all eternity. Bless you each and all.

Christos

This is Christos once again.

The spiritual vibrations within this community are at this time quite disturbed. There is much turmoil, much unrest, much unsettlement present in this area. People are becoming torn as to which direction to move their lives, as to which direction to pursue to continue their studies and growth. We do not wish to intimate that the vibrations level is becoming weaker or more negative within this area, for that is not true. We do say that it is a time of change. It is a weeding out process.

Many have begun their studies and have not pursued them with the proper motives and interests. They shall fall by the wayside for there is no time to play games. We cannot waste energies on those interested in creating phenomena, in creating notoriety for themselves, for the meager talents and tricks that they purport on others. If I sound a little stern, please forgive me. I only mean to accentuate the importance of what I am relating to you.

Many of you have committed yourself spiritually to your growth and to your path. You shall find your road perhaps harder but quicker, for all must be brought to awareness as rapidly as possible at this particular time. The need increases and grows every day. Do not allow yourselves to be deterred or swayed from your path by negative thought patterns that may try to invade your minds. Stand firm in your beliefs. Learn to recognize a force of energy that does not seem to be positive, and in your truth. Understand that the balancing forces shall increase their efforts to slow down conscious growth and development. The more the growth increases, the greater shall be their efforts, but the weaker shall become their energies for in the long analysis, Love always triumphs.

Questions and Answers

Being that tonight is the night of a full moon, we shall begin the question-and-answer period early. We shall save some time to bring each of you a message of a personal nature relating to your growth and your situation at this present time. Please proceed.

Question: I would like to know if the information I received on the hidden rainbow is true. If so, what am I to do with it? I have been told that all the colors from the rainbow brought together make the color black. We have muddied our own rainbow, that is why black is here. That is why we fear it, because we have produced it ourselves.

Answer: In one aspect this is true, but in the overall, it is not quite so. In general, spiritual interpretation, the color black denotes the absence of God's Light, and therefore, is not a color at all. In reality there is a level of energy which is a band of black light that serves as a shield of protection against higher rays of energy being exposed to those who are not capable of handling them. The black that is being produced that shadows some people is a product of their own development. It is a product of those who deny the existence of our Father, for they deny the existence of his Light and consequently of all color. They do not wish to bathe in His rainbow of Light.

Question: Could you tell us the possible metaphysical background for the ordinary childhood diseases and, perhaps why some do not undergo them until later in life?

Answer: You must understand that we cannot discount heredity, genes, and environment. By and large, the standard normal childhood diseases are just that. They truly do not have any correlation to any metaphysical lesson or karmic situation, except in rare cases where one suffers long term permanent effects from a disease and has chosen that as a lesson to experience.

Contagious disease is just contagious disease. Mankind has in the past, and shall again in the future, devise methods for controlling and eliminating diseases. We wish to tell you that mankind is on the verge, within the next twenty years of discovering a method for prolonging the life span of humanity. It shall come to pass within your lifetimes that man shall again live to one hundred and twenty years.

We shall begin to commence with the messages for all. Please listen carefully to each message, for each is truly for all of you. The energies pertain to some today, and some at a time not yet reached.

Blossom: You are at this time in your life, experiencing growth within the physical world. We realize that there is much turmoil in your life in relation to this, but you are doing very well. You are learning to separate the energies involved with the spiritual and the physical and use them in their proper perspective.

Do not have a reaction in a physical situation that is spiritual, nor mistake one for the other, for it would be difficult to handle. This is very often a difficult lesson for many to learn, for often one feels that if one is spiritual, one must react spiritually to all situations. Understand that you are in an existence of survival. One must do what is necessary to maintain one's position within society, and maintain the return flow of energies for energies expended. Your current situation shall come to a successful conclusion for you.

Armond: You are a very old soul, and yet it seems that for many years you have fought the emergence of your spiritual awareness. You have felt that it would cause an alteration or change within the structure of your life and is not yet comfortable for you. If it sounds plausible to you, we would suggest that when you meditate, to meditate upon your heart and feel the pulsations that come from this organ within your body and become sensitive to the vibrations that are within it. This shall help you greatly in your growth and under-standing. It shall bring you much needed peace.

Frances: You are indeed a Child of Light. You have kept your spiritual growth basically to yourself. I do not feel that you have reached the point within your confidence where you are ready to announce who you are, and begin to spread your truth to others, and so we ask you to take the plunge. You shall find that it becomes easy and far more rewarding for you. It is usually the first step that is the most difficult. This is what you are supposed to do, to share your Love and your vibrations with all you can reach. Have the faith and the confidence in yourself and all shall flow to you.

Ron: You are a very stubborn man. Part of your stubbornness is ac-tually a cover up for you. It puts you in a position of authority and dominance in a relationship. You are reaching a point where you are developing a desire to grow and become aware of yourself. For this we Bless you, but in order for you to grow you must soften the vi-brations and begin to allow others to be as they wish to be, without passing judgment and accepting and loving all as they present them-selves to you. Allow them to make their own mistakes. Then your growth shall commence in reality.

Marge: Every time we are in your vibrations, we feel a change and so we give you the confirmation of change. Your growth is moving along very nicely. We even ask you to slow down a little. Although you have a tremendous desire to absorb and learn, you must take time for assimilation and at times, to be a little more discriminating as to what you accept into your truth and philosophy. The growth shall come. I do not like to dwell on the word patience, but it does symbolize a process of filtering out and accepting in your mind your truth.

Ed: We ask you not to be concerned over your true love, for all shall come to pass. It is time for you to rebuild and conserve your energies for a while. The financial project you will soon embark on shall require great strength and protection, for there shall be much opposition to the completion of this mission. As you know, you shall receive all the back-up energy and support that will be necessary to complete the mission. It is a time when a financial structure must be established, and the funds made available for use by the Light workers. I confirm for you that the words we spoke to you earlier this week relating to this situation and the path laid out for you, are truth.

Warren: If you continue to grow as you are doing now, within a period of three years, you shall experience unification at the conscious level with your soul. All is falling into place for you now, and the reasons for the deprivation and uncertainty that you have experienced for many years shall become clearer to you every day. Those whose work it is to do total service for God, must, unfortunately feel the pangs of great deprivation at times, and great suffering to help increase and strengthen the Love within their vibrations that they may share it with others.

Judy: You are seated next to Warren, and the words I have to say to you are basically the words I have said to him. The only difference is that your spiritual work shall be behind the scenes, or in a type of supportive nature. You shall lend strength and organization to those who shall not have the time to do so for themselves. There is a highly concentrated degree of Love within your vibrations. It shall be used to support and encourage your brothers and sisters in their work and their growth, and for this, we Bless you.

Bonnie: Slowly but surely, the pieces of your life are falling into place for you. You are at a place in your development where you are experiencing old energies once more, for the last time. Some of them hurt, but it cannot be avoided. There is new strength permeating your vibrations. You shall be a teacher. Although this may seem far away to you now, your growth shall give you the confidence and the strength to teach others. You shall be involved within the area of numerology and its astrological correlations.

Robert: We do not have to tell you who you are for you know. We do recommend that periodically you get in your car and take a drive into the mountains, lay your spiritual work and thoughts aside, climb a mountain and just relax. Too much work creates imbalance. It is not expected of you or anyone, to devote 24 hours a day to your studies and growth. If it were so, you would be in spirit. Take time to relax and enjoy your life.

Marlene: You are undergoing a severe testing period at this time. The pressures within your job are increasing and making more and more demands upon your time. On the other side of the coin we have your growth, your desire to advance spiritually. So we say this to you. Do not allow guilt feelings to enter because of heavy pressures within your physical job. Understand that now this is where you must be. Remember that the energies relating to the physical must be completed before your true involvement with your spiritual growth can reach the higher levels. Do what you must and do it in peace.

Nancy: We congratulate you on your new vehicle. We realize that at times it seems that we are picking on you and giving you a difficult road to walk. Know that it is done in Love for your growth. There are some heavy things to overcome within your structure and within the regimentation of your mind. It is for this reason, and this reason alone, that many of the stages of growth that you have reached have seemed more difficult to reach. You are often your own worst enemy. The control of the logical, scientific mind is often difficult to release to allow the softer vibrations to enter. Have patience with us for we shall not give up.

Susan: You are in the finishing years of a cycle of much turmoil and heartache in your life. You have experienced this to build strength within your vibrations, to show you that you can experience these types of energies, and yet survive and rise above them. Your spiritual growth shall not be too conscious for a while as there are still things for you to accomplish physically. Do not feel that you are not growing, for indeed you are, it is only at the subconscious level. When the time arrives, the doors shall open to your consciousness and all the growth shall come to the surface. Then it shall be rapid and quite fulfilling for you.

Douglas: You are an alien soul. The strength in your voice is quite compatible with the strength in your vibrations. This means that your soul has chosen to incarnate on this planet for a series of incarnations of service for God. Your soul has experienced incarnations in more highly advanced civilizations. For this reason, your vibrations are more sensitive than many of your brothers and sisters. There are times that you shall feel uncomfortable in the presence of others, perhaps even consider yourself a misfit in society, but is is no more than a sensitivity of vibration.

You are here to perform tasks of a very specific nature within this incarnation. We shall give you some insight, but not too much. Most of it must develop from within you. You shall be involved within the structure of language interpretation relating to characters and symbols long lost and buried.

Jim: We ask you to search for peace within your soul. We ask you to understand that the things that you are experiencing within your life structure at this time, are part of your growth and development. Search behind the results of all situations you are involved in to find the cause and lesson involved with them. Many things have occurred to you within your life you have experienced more than once, for you have not taken the time to examine and understand them. If you will do this, you will find far more peace and it shall lead you to new growth and understanding of yourself.

Kathy: Do you have any children at this time? "No." One of the prime purposes for your incarnation involves the bearing of a child, a boy. His name shall be Johnathan, and you are here to serve as the vehicle for him to incarnate through. He is a very high soul that shall achieve much in the course of his lifetime. He shall be an extremely sensitive child. It shall be your responsibility to protect and nurture his vibrations. Your own growth shall precede his birth to prepare you for his arrival. You shall have a very warm, fulfilled, and loving life.

Madge: You are about to enter a level of initiation that will raise your vibrations substantially. In three or four weeks, whole new patterns of thoughts and energies shall begin to permeate your mind. We caution you to discern the information that comes to you and to keep an alert mind. All that shall come to you shall be Love, but much of it may come to you in the form of lessons. There will not be any suffering involved, only if you create it. It shall be completed in one year. At that time your conscious awareness shall have risen substantially.

Alice: You are at last returning to what it is you are to accomplish. Your vibrations have truly come to the surface within the past month and a half. It is believed that you have received the message that you are to resume your teaching and continue to do so. You must set aside time to pursue the writing of the several books that are within your mind, for these energies must become realistic and shared with others. We realize your schedule is quite heavy, and yet this work must be done for there are more books whose thoughts have not yet come to the surface in consciousness.

Jerry: The message we have for you this night is to realize that the search for your truth must take a different direction. Your study, your learning, your reading has served you well. Now the time has come for you to formulate your own truth from within. The answers you seek, the growth you desire, lies within you. Use the energies and the effort you are expending to pursue your education elsewhere to open doors from within, for only then shall you find your truth.

Virginia: You too have denied who you are. You have stunted your growth. Understand that we realize that it is sometimes difficult to take that step across the line and announce to the world, "here I am, here is my truth, listen to me, I bring you my truth." This removes the crutches and supports and leaves you standing by yourself, and yet, the time must come when the step must be taken, when the commitment to yourself must be total. You have much to offer and share with mankind and the time is overdue.

Janice: You have removed a shell from your body within the past month. It was a shell of constricting energy. Now you are free. You are happy. You are Light and Love. Never again allow yourself to be constricted or confined. Now your growth shall truly begin. You shall be a great healer, not only of body, but of mind and spirit. Your energies shall carry much Love to draw to you those who need you.

Suzanne: You are a sleeping child. The eyes are beginning to open, and the energies are beginning to flow. There are uncertainties and doubts within your vibrations, and that is good. It means that you will be careful and conservative. You shall not become frightened but shall grow and understand at your own rate and time. There are still many things for you to achieve within the physical area of your life. The hardships that you have experienced have not been accidental, but by and large they are over, for the lessons involved with them have been learned. The next year shall be a year of assimilation for you as well as a release from the past.

Pat: There is a light shining in your heart and the light has begun to spread and permeate your whole being, for you are indeed a Child of Light. The balance of your life shall be devoted to your spiritual path and your mission. There are a few areas relating to the physical that have not yet been consummated and are causing an irritation in your vibrations, but in three or four months all shall be flowing smoothly. You have made the choice and committed yourself to God's work, and the return of energy for this shall indeed, be ten-fold.

Regina: There is great strength in your vibrations. There is a tendency within you to shy away from situations due to past hurts and disappointments. We suggest that you eliminate that area of your vibrations, do a little self-analysis, try to understand the cause of the relationships and the lessons learned from them. When you have satisfied yourself, then you will no longer have any fears in those specific areas of your life. There is much yet for you to achieve within the physical vibrations of society, and for the time being, your growth shall be relegated to that of support of others. You shall come to the point where you shall decide to grow or not, for you have not yet determined that choice in your mind.

Carmen: All of your efforts and all of your work shall soon begin to bring you rewards. There shall be a clinic opening soon to care for those underprivileged people of your descent, that you may become associated with to do your healing and counseling with, for it is this area that you have been prepared for. You have shown much to those who have a need for your services. You have shown much patience and dedication, and for this you are truly blessed.

Stuart: Your vibrations have become much lighter and softer during the past year. We are pleased at the independence you have assumed in the areas of your spiritual growth. Over the years you have been denied much, to see if you could be deterred from your path, and yet you have not. There are times when you place your analytical mind in the way, but somehow when the growth is finally achieved it is more appreciated. There shall be an opportunity for you soon to relocate. We shall not offer any advice, only advise you that it shall arise.

I repeat the words that were stated to you earlier. Each of you, in their own right, has the ability and the capacity to become unified, at the conscious level, with your soul. Work towards it, strive for it. Then and only then, can you truly find love, peace and fulfill your mission for your Father.

And now, we still have some time left if there are any additional questions that have arisen.

Question: Can you explain how I deny who I am?

Answer: I do not say that you deny who you are to yourself. I say that you have not made others aware of who you are. It is desired that you expand your areas of involvement so that others may learn and share with you.

Question: Can you explain to me the super high energy I have been experiencing lately?

Answer: When one shares of onself to others and sees the results in the growth and understanding that develops, this energy is returned to the sender whose vibrations are increased, whose conscious Love flows to a greater degree. This is the purpose of teaching to learn, to grow. That is why we said to you that it is time for you to teach. These energies that you are experiencing shall continue to increase in vibration and shall always be with you.

Question: My brother is at a dramatic turning point in his life. Is there anything I can do to help him?

Answer: If he asks you for advice and help, you may offer it. If he does not ask, all you may do is send him love and strength that he may resolve these problems by himself. This is a lesson for him. There is much you could do to help him, but he must learn that it takes strength to ask for help, not weakness.

Question: The reports of my oldest son are negative. Is this negativity a part of his growth, or is it a deviation from it?

Answer: Your son is undergoing some heavy lessons at this time. He is not accepting the lessons. If he will learn to flow with events as they occur, the rest of his life will straighten out and flow for him. He must learn to accept his vibrations and work them through.

And now, it is time for us to draw this session for tonight to a close. Remember your responsibilities. Remember to make yourself available to all those who come to you in truth, seeking your advice, seeking your Light and your Love.

We Bless you for sharing with us this night.

We Bless you in the Divine Father's Name.

Chapter 16

Christos on Christmas

This is Christos. We Bless you.

The reason for the delay before the transmission has begun, was to try to shift away those spirits who have lined up to speak to you tonight. Since this is the last session for the year, many of your masters and teachers wish to say a few words to you. To Bless you for what you have achieved during this past year and to pray that you all continue your growth and your awareness as you have done this year, and so I speak to each one of you individually from your own masters to Bless you and to wish you well for the coming year.

We speak to you tonight on a topic that is quite dear to our hearts. We have titled it, and we call it, "Whatever happened to, and renewing the spirit of Christmas". All of you, without exception, are sitting here as if I have stabbed you in the heart, for all know what has happened to the spirit of Christmas, a commercial venture, a money making, degrading proposition where children grow up and their definition of Christmas is, "a day I get toys and presents". For adults it is a day they dread, for they must then look at next month's charge accounts for the bills they have accumulated. It is indeed sad.

I wish for you, you who walk in the Light, enjoyment in your Christmas this year. We sitting here, he and I who are as one, consider ourselves quite Blessed, for we carry the Christmas vibration with us all the time, as you all shall do in time.

Beginning eight days before the eve of Christmas day, which I believe is the sixteenth day of December, during your meditation, call for the Christ Spirit to emerge from your heart into your consciousness, to begin the celebration with you at that time. The world has forgotten that the purpose of Christmas is to be one with that vibration during that season.

This vibration is more predominant at that time than at any other time of the year. It is an opportunity for all to achieve a great level of growth during that time, to set a foundation for the new year, to begin to grow.

If I may make a suggestion, those of you within the circle who had planned to share with each other during this season and feel an obligation or desire to exchange presents, try to exchange your Love, your feelings towards a common interest and goal. This is a sharing that shall not be forgotten and shall be treasured always. Do not lower your standards by feeling obligated to others.

I look back into the vibrations of time, and I see the children of many generations ago, sitting and listening to stories. Stories of love and beauty, singing songs and sharing by the fire, happy to be sitting in a circle of Love. For them, it was the greatest present they could receive and share, for it had depth and substance.

Why must it be that only at Christmas time, on the birthday of Christ, mankind buys presents for himself? Is there a law that forbids mankind from buying presents on any normal day of the year, if he is buying them out of desire and love? Or has he become such a robot that he does what is expected of him because tomorrow is "the day"? Share with a friend whenever you wish. Buy them a present if you love them and because you love them, not because tomorrow is Christmas.

The spirit of Christmas is the Spirit of Christ. The energies of God are the energies of every Savior and Messiah that ever walked the face of this planet. These are the energies that burn within you at this time. Let us consider Christmas a rebirth for all of you, for indeed it is. Allow it to be the most joyous, spiritual day of the year. Believe that you will reap rewards on that day, for indeed you shall, as this is one purpose for Christmas: to receive the vibrations of Love.

Gather to you during this holiday season those souls who are alone and have none to share their joy with and be joyous with them. Share and spread your Love so that your sisters and brothers shall not be alone during this season.

The New Year is going to bring many many changes for all. Most of these changes have already begun to occur. Every month the vibrations of this circle are at a higher level than the preceding month and shall continue to grow along with the complexion of those you associate with and conduct your daily lives with.

There shall be new areas of information coming from higher levels of vibration. They shall open new vistas at the conscious level. Ancient languages, numerical systems and interpretations shall begin to flow to the surface, revealing many of the lost truths. You must be ready to handle them, to use them. It shall be a most rewarding, joyous year for you all.

I say to you once again, you are all Children of Light. If you were not, you would not be sitting in these vibrations. You would have entered this room, turned around and walked out for lack of compatibility with these vibrations.

All of you, without a single exception, have had an incident of substantial suffering during this past year. It shall not be so next year. Next year is an eighteen year, a year of life, eternal Love and growth. I would suggest that all of you look up the symbolic meaning behind the number eighteen. See what awaits you in the coming year, the challenges and the rewards.

I shall end my lecture at this time, for there is one other who wishes to express his energies through us, and there are many questions within the circle this night. God Bless you.

Newahjac: History of Creation

These are the energies of Newahjac, and we Bless you.

It has been several months since I have spoken to you. Let it suffice to say I have been away on a trip.

I want you all to understand that beginning next month, the beginning of the new year, my energies shall come to you every month through Christos, to bring to you a continuation of the lessons we have begun, relating to the history of Creation. I shall, from time to time, ask you to inquire into some reference material that I shall suggest, to further explanations and expansion on topics I shall discuss. If I do so, I would appreciate it if you would comply with my wishes.

If my voice seems stern, I must say to you that it is. I am not here to answer questions relating to anything other than what I am to teach. You have Christos for that purpose. My vibrations are channeled through a very fine protected screen, and it must remain that way. I wish to say that I am available for information to each and every one of you on an individual basis. However, if you call upon me to come to you and I am not there, know that you are not prepared for my arrival. By this I mean well rested, mind and body clear, and not weary. My energies are strong, and your body must be rested to carry my transmissions.

My name is spelled Newahjac. I am with the highest level of the Brotherhood. I only teach the Children of Light. Bless you all. I wish you much growth and send you Blessings for the new year that comes shortly. I send you your Divine Father's Blessings.

Questions and Answers

Now it is time for the period of questioning. We ask Stuart to please act as monitor.

Question: I would like confirmation on a soul change. Yes, or no?

Answer: The soul change has occurred, yet you are not totally aware consciously of all aspects of it. You have only become aware of part of the change of your vibrations. If the total change were to come upon you all at once, it would have caused you great discomfort and distress, what you have experienced is partial. The balance shall come to you slowly, and your level of awareness shall increase far beyond its present level.

Question: I returned to Phoenix over route #10 from New Mexico. When I crossed the state border there were some mountains on the left. As I passed, I felt a surge of energy greater than I have experienced anywhere else I have been. It lasted all the way into Phoenix. Has there been an appreciable increase of energy into this area?

Answer: Yes, and it shall continue to increase.

Question: I feel that I should return to these mountains.

Answer: We would suggest that you shelve those vibrations for a while. Not to dismiss them from your mind, only to shelve them. There are more important things for you to concern yourself with at this time. The vibrations in this area shall continue to increase in preparation for the change of the basic Earth vibrations in only four years. More and more, your sisters and brothers shall be flocking to this area, bringing their vibrations with them. You shall find a large influx of Children of Light from California to this area next year. Those who have grown will realize that they need to come here to continue their growth in the vibrations of higher truth.

Now is a time for you to reassimilate your energies, to gather yourself together, to settle in your mind what has happened to you in the past year. Place it in the proper perspective for your own growth.

Question: I live a little north and east. Every night I see two large ships. Could they be verbally identified?

171

Answer: They are Jupiter I and Jupiter 70.

Question: Could you tell me something about the word, "Aohm?

Answer: The word Aohm, spelled AOHM, is commonly referred to as a Universal sound. It contains all movements of the mouth that would be used in speaking any of the characters of your language. Its function is to create a vibration, and also to achieve this vibration within you when you are in a contemplative or meditative state. Each Child of God carries with them their own mantra, or sound. A sound according to their own level of vibration. This mantra does not remain with the individual for their entire lifetime. It changes as the individual grows and responds to a higher sound.

Question: Can you give me some advice as to what I can do in relation to my father's illness at this time?

Answer: You do not need to understand, just understand. However, you can help in a different way. It is your role in this situation to send Love and energies to your father. You cannot become physically involved. You can only understand, for this is the way it must be. This may not be enough of an answer for you, but you shall understand in a few days. Many times, when we are involved in a family, we draw guilt to ourselves, especially if we are away from them, and allow old emotional problems to emerge. This creates the need to understand, and forces us to ask why, instead of accepting the situation and having faith.

Question: I have begun to study the Hebrew alphabet, and I was wondering if it is good for me to continue doing so, or should I spend my time on other things?

Answer: We are pleased that you have begun to re-study the Hebrew alphabet. If you believe it is something you want to do, then you must do it. It shall certainly assist you in recall and in your growth.

172

Question: Could you tell me about Mephisto?

Answer: Mephisto is one of the Ancients. He is currently serving as an Ascended Master who no longer incarnates and serves in the capacity of working with selected Children of Light to increase their knowledge in specific areas of philosophy.

Question: How may I find out what my personal mantra is?

Answer: All you have to do is ask.

Question: What is my personal mantra, please?

Answer: Your mantra is Ra-Aohm.

Question: Could you tell us if there will be a crash in the economy of the U.S.? If so, when?

Answer: We do not believe there will be a collapse of the economy in this country. We do believe that there will be a serious recession for a period of time. The next recession will be more severe. Understand that there shall be many many changes. Do not dwell on these matters. Think about what you can achieve in growth this day and tomorrow. That is your reality. Do not feed on negativity, nor concern yourself with it. If everyone would do this, all would be resolved and well.

Question: Can you offer me some guidance in my life?

Answer: The best guidance we can offer you is not to be overwhelmed by all the situations and questions that come into your mind. They cause insecurities and lack of confidence in your own abilities. Try to handle them one at a time. You have much room for growth, and much growth to come to the conscious level. Have faith in yourself. Write down your questions and discuss them with us at the conscious level. We shall be pleased to discuss them with you.

Question: I would like to know if there is anything more I can do to heal the physical damage to my body, as well as the re-alignment of my body energies?

Answer: We suggest that you use the ray of violet and lavender, specifically in the area of your back. The re alignment of your energies is taking place slowly. Realize that your system received quite a shock. We are pleased at the progress you have already made. Your determination and dedication shall not go in vain.

Question: Could you tell me if the papers I gave you last week are valid and in truth?

Answer: I would like to say that I am surprised that you ask me such a question. You know as well as I do that, they are valid. However, I realize the importance of a confirmation now and then, even for a master. All is valid, all is truth.

Question: I'm contemplating a move. It involves one or two parties. Would this move be good for me, or would it inhibit my growth?

Answer: If the move is good for you, it will not inhibit your growth. If the move is not good for you, it will inhibit your growth. Both answers are valid.

This is not something we wish to comment on. It is a free will decision relating to your physical involvements with others. It is a part of your growth and your lessons. Listen to yourself. Follow your intuition and you shall make the proper decision.

Question: Have I reason to fear (Name) and his machine? I have been using the 29th ray to protect myself. Is it adequate?

Answer: The ray is not being penetrated by this person. However, we caution you to maintain your protection. We are not comfortable with this situation. You are aware enough to make your own decisions. When you listen to others you realize your mistakes. Have the confidence in youself. It shall smoothen out your life.

174

There are certain people this night that I wish to introduce to each other as part of being as one. When I call their names, I wish them to stand: Hayden, Gail, Alyce, Maxine, Janice, Judith, Lanita, and Blossom.

You are all sisters, now and for the balance of your lives. You may be seated, please. There shall always be a unity of your vibrations. The circle shall increase as more are added.

If there are no more questions then we shall end this session for this night, for this year, for this vibration in Love.

We wish you all continued growth. We wish you Love, health and happiness. This coming year shall find us in a circle of new Light and vibrations. Our numbers shall grow and grow.

We Bless you and Love you with the energies of our Divine Father.

We Bless you all.

Books Frank Alper

Exploring Atlantis Vol. 1, Vol.2, Vol. 3 combined (from 1981 – 1986)
ISBN 978-1-4475-4994-9

Our Existence is Mind, Healing Methods for the 3rd Millennium.
ISBN 978-3-9524451-2-9

A series of spiritual lectures channeled through the Soul of Rev. Frank Alper D.D.:

Moses and the Bible Vol. 1 (1980) ISBN 978-3-9524930-8-3

Moses and the Bible Vol. 2 (1980) ISBN 978-3-9524930-9-0

Moses and the Bible Vol. 3 (1982) ISBN 978-3-9526044-0-3

Moses and the Bible Vol. 4 (1982) ISBN 978-3-9526044-1-0

A series of spiritual lectures channeled through the Soul of Rev. Frank Alper D.D.:

An evening with Christos Vol. 1 (Sept. 1978 – Dec. 1979
ISBN 978-3-9526044-2-7
An evening with Christos Vol 2 (Jan. – Dec. 1980)
ISBN 978-3-9526044-3-4
An evening with Christos Vol 3 (Jan. – Dec. 1981
ISBN 978-3-9526044-4-1
An evening with Christos Vol 4 (Jan. – Dec. 1982)
ISBN 978-3-9526044-5-8
An evening with Christos Vol 5 (Jan. – Dec. 1983)
ISBN 978-3-9526044-6-5

SOUL PLAN by Blue Marsden

RECONNECT WITH YOUR TRUE LIFE PURPOSE

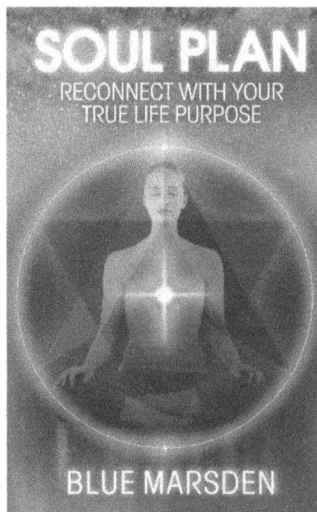

'Soul Plan' is a new interpretation of an ancient system of life purpose analysis. Available now to a wider audience, this method accesses the vibration in your birth name, to determine your entire soul plan.

Moses conveyed the method of Numerology to Dr. Frank Alper, who documented it in Volume 2 of this series. Dr. Alper named this system "The Spiritual Numerology of Moses." Later, he received additional insights and updated the symbols, which are now used by practitioners and students.

In "Soul Plan," Blue Marsden has meticulously compiled and expanded these teachings into a volume that has captivated readers globally and is available in multiple languages. This authoritative guide, enriched with numerous charts and examples, spans 400 pages and is an invaluable resource for anyone seeking a deeper understanding of their soul's journey.

ISBN: 978-1781800768
Length: 400 pages

Embark on a transformative journey today with "Soul Plan" and discover the divine blueprint of your life.

www.ingramcontent.com/pod-product-compliance
Lightning Source LLC
Chambersburg PA
CBHW052044090426
42739CB00010B/2038